THE POLITICS OF EVERYDAY LIFE IN GĨKŨYŨ POPULAR MUSIC OF KENYA (1990-2000)

MAINA wa MŨTONYA

TWAWEZA
COMMUNICATIONS
"Working Towards a Better World"

Published in 2013 by:
Twaweza Communications Ltd.
P.O. Box 66872 - 00800 Westlands
Twaweza House, Parklands Road
Mpesi Lane, Nairobi Kenya
website: www.twawezacommunications.org
Tel: +(254) 020 269 4409

Design and Layout: Catherine Bosire
Cover design: Franciscan Kolbe Press
Cover Photo: Maina Mũtonya

ISBN: **978-9966-028-44-0**

Printed by:
Franciscan Kolbe Press
P.O. Box 468, 00217 Limuru, Kenya
Email: press@ofmconvkenya.org

DEDICATION

In the memory of my late dad, Mūthee Mūtonya wa Njūgūna (November 27th 1933 - January 7th 2004), my mentor, friend and father whose inspiration has propelled me all along; to you, the book is dedicated. Thanks for watching over me in my every move. *Ūromama kwega kuraga.*

And to the rest of my family: Maitū Njoki, Mūthee Mūtonya, Njūgūna, Kamenjū, Mūngai, Wangūi, Marī, Wanjirū, Kamau, Mūciiri, Mwangi (Soja), Mūkami and Machīra, plus the rest of the Mūtonya extended family.

CONTENTS

ABOUT THE AUTHOR

Maina wa Mũtonya, from Kenya, is currently a research professor at the Center for Asian and African Studies at El Colegio de México, in México, charged with the responsibility of teaching African Literature, African Philosophy and Swahili. He obtained his PhD degree in African Literature and Cultures from the University of the Witwatersrand, South Africa. His most recent publications (articles) include *"La Negociación de Identidades Urbanas en el Mũgithi y la Ejecución de One-Man Guitar en Kenia"* (2012) *The Beat Goes on: Performing Postcolonial Disillusionment in Kenya* (2010) and *"Fimbo ya Nyayo: When the Dictator Called the Tunes"* (Forthcoming). He was a co-author in **Retracing Kikuyu Music** (2010), a multimedia project by Ketebul Music comprising a book, documentary DVD and audio CD. His research interests include popular culture and politics in Africa, literature and performance of power in post-independence Africa, identity formation in popular culture in Africa, specifically Kenya and Gĩkũyũ and Swahili languages. His current research interests include a study of the politics of remembering, violence and representation in the popular cultural terrain of Kenya. He is presently a member of the African Literature Association, the Africa Studies Association and the International Society for African Philosophy and Studies.

ACKNOWLEDGEMENTS

For a journey that took off in a small muddy nursery school in Gatūra village, it would be practically impossible to mention everybody who has made this endeavour a success. For those in love with learning more about our traditions and cultures, the journey has just begun, in earnest!

This project has been a process, duly informed by my upbringing in Gatūra in Gatanga division, in Central Province, Kenya, a region that has been home and continues to produce the largest percentage of Gīkūyū musicians over the years.

But more importantly, my parents, Maitū Njoki and Mūthee Mūtonya have always been an inspiration. With their unfailing commitment to transmit to us the heritage and custom of the Gīkūyū, they have remained the oral historians of our community at all times. It is through their avid love for music, both local and international that provided much fodder for this research. The constant interaction with my siblings too as regards our music has continually offered fresh insights into the understanding of our culture.

Thus, to my brothers, sisters, nieces and nephews from all corners of the world, who have always been very supportive to me throughout the years, this book is in your honor.Thanks for the encouragement and support; material, moral and spiritual. The ancestors have actually acknowledged our numerous droplets of libation poured every now and then. FacingMt. Kenya, the prayers have definitely reached *Mwene Nyaga*. I say *Thaai*.

My appreciation too goes to our musicians, whose responsibility as the voices of the voiceless they continually carry out against all odds!

This book project has also benefited generously from the guidance, support and encouragement, especially during the course of conducting research over the years. I remain forever indebted to professors Joyce Nyairo, Evan Mwangi, Kīmani Njogu, James Ogude, Peter Kagwanja and Ketebul Music under Tabu Osusa for their contribution towards actualizing this research into a book. Thank you for being part of my academic extended family, together with my colleagues from Moi University, University of the Witwatersrand and El Colegio de Mexico.

Putting the best forward, let us only remember that, *mwomboko ti hinya, no makinya meerī na kuuna!*

PREFACE

This study is situated in the post-1990 years – rightly depicted as an age of major sociopolitical transformations and upheavals, of the momentous collapse of the Cold-War order, which also ushered in the struggles to create a 'new' order. This book fills an important gap by adeptly using popular music as a form of political oppression and the musician as a critical social player to understand the intricacies of Kenya's turbulent politics in the crucial 1990s and after. Mūtonya shows that popular music is that which is consumed by the majority and is connected to the lives of people.

The significance of this book, however, is not in the manner it shows how popular music works to expose the ugly face of officialdom but rather in its compelling insights into how popular music works to create those rare moments of freedom, away from those regulated zones of officialdom. In this sense, the author demonstrates how popular music provides the space for performing alternative politics, not only for the underclass but also for the middle class who under an authoritarian regime of Daniel arap Moi in the decade under study are often provided with limited avenues of expression.

The author correctly notes that urbanization, commercialization and globalization have contributed to the vibrancy of Gĩkũyũ popular music of the 1990s which is marked by hybridity, syncretism and innovativeness. It is a product of social processes and cannot be separated from society, politics and 'the burning issues of the day'. The music expresses social cosmology, worldviews, class and gender relations, interpretations of value systems and other political, social and cultural practices, even as it entertains and relaxes its audience. It is a window into the life of society and an illuminator of reality.

There is a specific focus on *benga* musicians, especially Joseph Kamarũ, Joseph Kariũki, Albert Gacherũ and *Mũgithi* artists. The developments discussed regarding Kenya also resonate with other parts of Africa, giving the book a distinct cross-regional and multidisciplinary edge and usefulness. From a broad methodological viewpoint, this research is competently secured on the popular music of the Gĩkũyũ – a key ethnic group at the epicenter of Kenya's power politics.

This provides a useful and manageable case study of the larger and complex political realities that the Kenyan/Gĩkũyũ musician and music have sought to represent. The book also ably harnesses evidence from field research and from an array of published works to successfully making the powerful case that music, as an aspect of popular culture, has served as an effective agent of political change, which has also been refashioned by the changing social and political dynamics and realities of the decade of the 1990s.

CHAPTER ONE

Introduction

Gĩkũyũ music in Kenya: A Historical Background

Owing to its multi-ethnic composition, popular music in Kenya undoubtedly enjoys a wide diversity in terms of styles and beats. The intra and inter-ethnic collaborations as well as healthy interactions between the local and the foreign and the modern and the traditional have enhanced the popular music of this country. Therefore, what is presently referred to as the popular music in Kenya is the embodiment of this cultural diversity that Kenya enjoys. Of the many cultural varieties that are alive in Kenya, this research picks on the popular music of the Gĩkũyũ community in investigating how popular culture, in this instance, popular music, forms an integral part in the expression of everyday life. In this critical analysis, the research provides the historical background of the music and how the popular music of the Gĩkũyũ people between 1990 and 2000 as a cultural production that has portrayed the daily struggles, hopes, aspirations, impediments, desires, disillusionment, anxieties and fears of everyday life of this Kenyan community.[1]

The period 1990-2000 witnessed in Kenya significant and crucial changes in the lives of the Kenyans, ranging from the political, economic, social to cultural realms as will seen in preceding chapters. In analysing the popular music of the Gĩkũyũ and significance of the moment of production, this research imperative is an effort towards 'seeking to understand them as expressions of particular individuals or groups, and also as generalized responses to desire, need, loss, or misery, as expressions of joy and elation' (Agawu, 2001:3) during the dislocating moments represented by the decade 1990-2000.

While this study is on Gĩkũyũ popular music, it does not preclude the existence of other popular cultural forms and practices among the various communities during this period. Rather, it is for purposes of specificity and scope of this research, which may otherwise prove unmanageable given the diverse nature of multi-ethnic Kenya[2], that this research is focused solely on the study of the Gĩkũyũ popular music. Among other objectives, this will also be an exploration of the discourses and themes that prevail in the music. Inescapably, therefore, the stylistic choices made by the musicians to capture and retain the audiences inform this study. Notions of intertextuality as discussed later are prevalent in the musical discourse, both in the studies and in the music itself. The study involves contextualising music, one as an aspect of popular culture and, second, as a text. It is important at this stage to provide a historical background to the Gĩkũyũ community as well as growth and development of their popular music.

The Gĩkũyũ community and their music

Gĩkũyũ is the language spoken by the Gĩkũyũ people who number about 7 and a half million and make up the largest ethnic group in Kenya. Recent figures indicate that the population of Kenya is at 40,046,566. The Gĩkũyũ constitute about 22% of this population.[3]

The Europeans from the Swahili inhabitants of the Coast coined the word Kikuyu. As Cristiana Pugliese[4] rightly notes, the proper spelling should be Mũgĩkũyũ (singular), Agĩkũyũ (plural for the people), Gĩkũyũ for their country and Gĩgĩkũyũ for the language. It is only for simplicity and convention that the language is called Gĩkũyũ. In that case, the term "Gĩkũyũ" can either 'mean the language or the people; it is also used adjectively. As for non-Kikuyu speakers, 'they invariably employ the term "Kikuyu", whether they mean the people, the language or when they use it adjectively' (Wanjohi, 1997:33). This study has employed the term "Gĩkũyũ" and Kikuyu interchangeably to denote both the language and the people.

The Gĩkũyũ in Kenya inhabit the Central Province in Kenya and seven administrative districts; Thika, Murang'a, Maragwa, Nyeri, Kiambu, Kirinyaga, and Nyandarua. Murang'a, which is in the middle, is traditionally considered to be the ancestral land of the Gĩkũyũ people. The community also constitutes a significant proportion of migrant communities in Nairobi because of the proximity to the capital (which was in pre-colonial times, a Maasai area)[5] and the Gĩkũyũ are also present in considerable numbers in other areas around Kenya, and a sizeable population in the Diaspora.

Most of the musicians in this research inquiry use the Gĩkũyũ language in their music. Pugliese (1995:84) reminds us that the language has been used to 'transmit complex ideas from ancient times, as Kikuyu oral literature is rich in riddles and proverbs; let alone the fact that written Gĩkũyũ has been used to explain complex religious concepts (translations of the Bible and commentaries), and also to express modern political concepts in the vernacular press'.

Presently, there are three Gĩkũyũ broadcasting stations, Kameme FM, Inooro FM and Coro FM that initially broadcast in Nairobi and the Mt. Kenya region where majority of the Gĩkũyũ people reside.[6] They address quite successfully the aesthetic need of their audience, the Gĩkũyũ, by broadcasting in a language majority of their listeners understand and play music which is identifiable in the region.

The choice of the Gĩkũyũ popular music[7] is both strategic, owing to ideas of accessibility both to the music and of the language to the researcher, and imperative for the following reasons. The Gĩkũyũ is the most populous community in Kenya and their music constitutes quite a large audience. It is a fact that they populate most parts of Nairobi city.

Walking down the busy River Road in downtown Nairobi, (was called 'little Murang'a'[8] in the 70s) the hub of music studios, rarely would one miss a Gĩkũyũ song blaring loud. In fact, The Simba Centre on River Road is home to many production and distribution houses of the Gĩkũyũ music, both secular and gospel. This is music whose audience is not only the Gĩkũyũ, but also appeals to other communities, just like the Gĩkũyũ people would form part of the audience of music from other regions. The audiences of this music transcend the ethnic barriers and the music becomes a symbol of the struggles of 'everyday life', through its beats and lyrics. As Bender (1991: xiii) rightly asserts, African music is more than just the musical sounds. A poignant reminder in Kenyan cultural scene is Eric Wainaina's song, *Rĩtwa Rĩaku* (Gĩkũyũ: Your Name) that is sung in Gĩkũyũ, and backed up with western brass and percussion instruments. Surprisingly, this folkloric number has appealed not just to the Gĩkũyũ ethnic group, but also to all groups, thereby transcending ethnic boundaries[9]. This is just one example that supports the argument that music has an enduring ability to affect us, often to withstand the test of time and to transcend the limitations of its particular, historical and cultural locations.

However, while the Gĩkũyũ make up Kenya's largest ethnic group, the audience for their music has always circulated mostly around this community. But this is not to imply that the musicians have not recorded resounding successes in their careers. Some of these include Joseph Kamaru, D.K. wa Maria, Wahome Maingi, CDM Kiratu, John Ndichu, Francis Rugwiti, Lawrence Nduru amongst others, from the 1970s to the present moment. In the 1980s and 1990s, successful names have included Musaimo, Queen Jane, John De Mathew, Mwalimu James Mbugua, Mukaramani, Peter Kigia, Joseph Kariuki, Joseph Wamumbe, Albet Gacheru, Sammy Muraya and many others. The late 1990s into 2000s saw the entrant of 'one-man' guitarists like Mike Murimi, Mike Rua and Salim Junior, as well as 'one-lady' guitarist, Wangari wa Kabera. This research only concentrates on secular music, but also acknowledges the existence of an equally extensive body of gospel music that spans decades, in the Gĩkũyũ community.

But what is referred to as popular music in this research project has been in existence from as early as the 1940s with musicians like Gachungi, John Arthur, HM Kariuki, Wanganangu and many others, who are beyond the scope of this study presently. However, one musician who has been in the trade from as early as the 1960s to the present day is Joseph Kamaru. An analysis of his music appears in later chapters. In 1967, Kamaru registered his presence on the Kenyan popular music scene with songs that appropriated the *benga* beat, but misc that also had an affinity to country music. As will be seen later, Kamaru's forte is his mastery of the Gĩkũyũ language in his songs, whether in social or political themes.

The appreciation of contemporary Gĩkũyũ popular music in scholarly discourses in Kenya, unlike other cultural productions like theatre, has received little or no attention. Scant popular culture studies on Kenya mention the music in passing despite the subject's nuanced articulation of the daily struggles about life, just like in many other literary and cultural artefacts. When the studies have been done [the few that there is], apart from recent studies on the hip-hop culture hitting most third world youth, the music of the 60s and 70s dominate the pages. One or two references acknowledge the contribution of both Joseph Kamaru and Daniel 'DK' Kamau. But the 1990s have seen quite a proliferation of skilled and sturdy musicians with powerful lyrics as well as inventive stylistic choices[10]. This research analyses music from the following

Gĩkũyũ musicians: Albert Gacheru, Jane Nyambura (Queen Jane), Joseph Kariuki, Joseph Kamaru, Eric Wainaina, Peter Kigia, *Mũgithi* artists Mike Rua, Mike Murimi and Salim Junior.

The peripheral status of Kenyan popular musicians in, scholarly works just like in most parts of Africa probably arises from the musicians' locale in society. As Stapleton and May (1989) argue, musicians are traditionally viewed as vagabonds, drunkards and reprobates. They exemplify the case of renowned benga artiste of the 1960s and 1970s, Daniel Owino (D.O) Misiani, 'whose father broke his first guitar, confiscated a second and went as far as begging the village authorities to arrest his errant son'[11] (1989:233). Albert Gacheru, one of the singers who is part of this study, had a similar experience. During school holidays, he would compose songs secretly because his parents were opposed to his engagement in music and wanted him to concentrate on his studies. His parents also believed that musicians were a wayward lot who could come to no good. Then one day, it came as a surprise to his parents when they heard their son's songs over the radio.

Though the period under study is 1990-2000, it is prudent to touch on traditional genres of the Gĩkũyũ music, which has inevitably provided inspiration for modern day artists. The genres were mostly classified on gender and age terms. *Nduumo* was a women's dance, a form replete with sexual connotations. *Kĩbaata* was a male dance for young warriors and mostly included songs of victory and praises. *Gĩtiiro* was done by elderly women after the dowry to celebrate the expansion of their clan. There was also *Mũthĩrĩgũ, Mũcũng'wa, Gĩcaandĩ* and *Mwomboko*. Some of these forms have filtered into the contemporary music of the Gĩkũyũ. *Mwomboko* was a kind of waltz for both men and women. The interaction with the West modified some forms like *Mwomboko*, which is nowadays accompanied by an accordion. One of the present greatest exponents of *Mwomboko* is H.M. Kariuki.

The different forms of the songs appealed to different themes. This depended on the time or the season when it was created and performed and the prevailing circumstances within the society. The *Mwomboko* and *Mũthĩrĩgũ* of 1940s were triggered by the animosity between the Gĩkũyũ people and the colonisers. In the 1960s, the same forms, especially *Mwomboko* were used to castigate the rise of neo-colonialism, and highlighted the post-independence disillusionment, and lack or recognition to freedom fighters. Kamaru's song, *Hũrĩra Tindo* (Drive the Chisel) illustrates the situation:

> *Rĩrĩa mũkũrĩa na mũkanyua* – When you are dining and wining
> *Mũkĩgũraga matoyota* – as you buy Toyotas
> *Nacio nding'ũri macindĩci* - and tycoons buy Mercedes
> *Nyũmba ya Mũmbi* – House of Mũmbi[12]
> *Nĩmwariganĩirwo nĩ Kĩmathi* – you have completely forgotten Kĩmathi[13].

From this excerpt, we can glean class differences as well as the postcolonial disillusionment in Kenya, immediately after independence. It, therefore, becomes clear that songs respond to the prevailing circumstances at that particular moment. It is, thus, unviable to classify these traditional songs as serving specific functions.

In 1921, Harry Thuku, the leader of the workers movement in colonial Kenya was arrested and about 150 people killed at a march demanding his release. Mary Nyanjiru led women in a confrontation with the colonial police on university way. That moment was captured in the *Kanyegenyũri* songs of the 1920s. It was to be recaptured again in the *Mũthĩrĩgũ* songs.

The Kikuyu independents in the 1930s used songs as a cultural tool to resist the ban on female circumcision by the colonial authorities. The most popular among these was *Mũthĩrĩgũ* that was sung for the uncircumcised girl. The songs depicted the new convert girls who had foregone circumcision as irresponsible, morally loose and lacking in discipline.

The traditional forms of the Gĩkũyũ, as with other communities, therefore, performed several functions: they were reflectors of a people's philosophy and aesthetics; a medium of culture; a source of entertainment; a historical record, and could be used to castigate wrongdoers and enhance positive behaviour.[14] The conclusion one can draw from the above, therefore, is that, song, dance and music have always been part and parcel of the day-to-day living of most communities.

Whereas there is a Gĩkũyũ variant of *benga*, some musicians still appropriate traditional modes of music. Kamaru is well known for his *Mwomboko* (a variant of waltz or tango)[15] beats while Queen Jane Nyambura borrows heavily from *Mũcũng'wa*. Worth noting, however, is that most musicians have stuck to the *benga* beat, which involves mostly the use of the guitar. Though the beat may sound very monotonous, the lyrics are quite rich and informative.

Despite all the foreign influence Kenyan music has a number of its own distinct and highly exuberant forms. *Taarab* in the coast a Muslim orchestral music, and *beni* stretches back to early years of the century. Other traditional forms also existed amongst the different communities. As earlier noted, the existence of music instruments like harps and lyres, drums amongst others, attests to this. Such forms of traditional music have formed a rich repertoire from where even modern popular musicians draw their inspiration. These formed part of music as well as dance rhythms.

Various Gīkūyū artists have inculcated the traditional forms into their popular music. Jane Nyambura, popularly known as Queen Jane in the Kenyan music scene includes traditional folk form *Mūcūng'wa* within contemporary Gīkūyū pop. Most of her albums covers feature her dressed in traditional attire of the Gīkūyū community; in *mūthuru*, which was a skirt made of skin, and huge earrings, known as *hang'i*.

Harrison Ngunjiri, popular known as Hardstone exemplifies the fusion between Gīkūyū folk music and western rap. From his CD, *Nuting but de Stone*, his hit song *Ūhiki* (wedding) appropriates Marvin Gaye's *Sexual Healing*, at least in the beat, but relies heavily on Gīkūyū folk in the lyrics, fused with rap.

Joseph Kamaru is also known for his affinity to country music. Most of his album covers portray him much in the same light as western cowboys and country musicians. Donned in a wide brimmed hat and jean suits, one would easily confuse him with the famous country musician, Jimmy Rogers[16]. His music too gains from the country music genre, but he is well known for fusing Gīkūyū traditional folk forms with contemporary trends.

Perhaps Joroge Benson's music stands out as the only Gīkūyū reggae and raga musician in the decade that this research focuses on. Joroge translates some of the earlier Gīkūyū songs, like Kamaru's *Jimmi* and *Hūrīra Tindo* (Drive the Chisel) and replays them with a style reminiscent of Caribbean reggae calypso star Yellow man. Joroge has his own collection of songs both in Gīkūyū and English, all of them with a heavy leaning towards reggae and dancehall.

Notes Paterson (1999: 519):

> Over the last few years, many of Kenya's ... musicians have taken inspiration from rap, R&B, house reggae and dancehall genres, blending elements of Euro-American pop with local Kenyan melodies, lyrics and rhythms.

However, what is quite distinct in most of this new blend of music is the omnipresence of the *benga* beat throughout. Secondly, even with the advanced music instruments, the guitar remains the dominant force in most of this music, in this case, Gĩkũyũ popular music. Thirdly, the traditional folk forms form a template onto which this new music is founded on. Various examples quoted above attest to this. The music under study deals with a whole range of themes and subjects as will be seen in the following chapters. The thematic concerns point to the daily struggles of everyday life.

Popular music in Kenya

Popular music in Kenya at best can be described as a mixture between the local and the foreign; 'the outside and indigenous, regional sounds'.[17] However, it must not be lost to researchers in music, the existence of a rich musical culture in the pre-colonial societies in Kenya and Africa at large. The interaction and eventual crossbreed with the West only led to a modification of the existing ethnic sounds. The tradition of music has of late laid a strong foundation onto which modern musicians regularly borrow from. I return to this discussion in a short while.

The 1950s in Kenya formed an epochal niche, which gave birth to the pop music we listen to at present in Kenya. The flow of music from the then Zaire (presently known as the Democratic Republic of Congo) began in the 1950s with the acoustic guitars and continued throughout the 1960s and 1970s 'when émigré bands took the Kenya club scene and recording business by storm' (Stapleton and May 1989:226). The end of the Second World War too had a great influence in the development of what we refer to here in this study as the beginnings of modern pop music in Kenya, when, 'Kenyan soldiers, returning from the front brought back disposable cash, guitars and accordions' (*ibid*). Gramophones became popular, and so did GV records, which had strong influences on East

African musician. With these influences, came about a distinctive African urban music.

The arrival of the new instruments, added to the tradition of the stringed instruments in most pre-colonial societies in Kenya[18] led to an emergence of new guitar styles. The new styles also benefited greatly from the early 1960s arrival of electric bands, 'some playing imitations of Zairean rumba, others western pop and a form of African twist which leant heavily on the new electrified *kwela*[19] guitar sound from South Africa' (Stapleton and May, 1989:229). Fadhili Williams's greatest classic of all times, *Malaika* itself was like a slow *rumba*.

Despite a brief stint of songs recorded in the *lingua franca*, Swahili immediately after independence, the Congolese influence on the local music was hard to ignore, both in Kenya and Tanzania. However, the mid-1970s witnessed the emergence of a local distinctive Kenyan beat in the shape of *benga*. Though it had been popularized in the 1960s by the likes of George Ramogi and D.O. Misiani[20], the 70s saw the beat offer stiff competition to the rumba dominance. Though specifically a beat from western Kenya, mostly from the Luo and Luhya communities, other groupings followed suit: Stapleton and May, (1989:231) comment:

> While the Luos followed root rhythms, Kikuyu musicians [from central Kenya] like Joseph Kamaru, with his City Sounds, and Francis Rugwiti developed their own vernacular sound that took much of its sweetness and bounce from American country and western, Jimmy Rogers being particularly influential, while the Kamba band, the Kilimambogo Boys, created their own mesmerizing *benga* sound, keyed around instrumental patterns and frequent rhythm-guitar breaks.

The fast spread of *benga* to other parts of Kenya and development of the various variation meant that artists like Kamaru and Kilimambogo boys had always to have musical backing from Luo guitarists. Most of the Gĩkũyũ music in this study thus falls under the *benga* style.

Though the *benga* influence has to large extent influenced the styles of many a popular musicians in Kenya, there is also a significant impact of styles and beats of international origin. Such examples, as noted earlier on, include the Western country music. The adaptation of style, notwithstanding, the use of Kenyan local vernaculars gives the music the local flavour.

Regional musicians, especially from the Democratic Republic of Congo, Tanzania, Uganda and other neighbouring states have also redefined popular Kenyan music. By using the Swahili language[21], it is intended that the music will reach a wider audience in the east and central African region. However, given the success of Lingala[22] music in Kenya over the years, one would argue that not all musicians play to a regional or an ethnic audience. D.K wa Maria´s romantic song *I Love You*, done in the Gĩkũyũ language was a national hit in multi-ethnic Kenya in the 1970s, in the same way as GidiGidi MajiMaji´s politically-loaded *Unbwogable,* (mostly in Luo language), was popular in 2002.

With increased interaction between the West and the rest, hip-hop, largely a black American musical form has found itself in the studios of many an African country. Hip-hop forms a great research imperative, which is beyond the scope of this research.

It is difficult to talk of a whole continent's music or a country's music without starting from the individual communities that make up a country/ continent. The term African music is deceptive in the sense that there exist distinct and diverse genres and types of music amongst the Africans. As Bender rightly comments, 'each ethnic group has its own music and the astounding wealth of musical creativity in Africa is not [and should not] be easily reduced to a common denominator'. This is a view amplified by Chernoff (1979:30) who argues:

> Although to discuss African music or African anything will involve the looseness and possible distortions that comes with generalizations, we realize that without a general meaning and order of what we may see and hear at an African musical event, it would be difficult to sense the significance of the variety of specific details we may experience.

Veit Erlmann's (1999:8) argument in the above discussion throws in more light on the subject of music and identity. He feels strongly that Africans and Europeans have represented each other for centuries, if not millennia, through a variety of media and objects, imagining common spaces and narratives. To him, 'it therefore follows that no "local identity" can ever be construed from the grounds circumscribed purely by a bounded defined place'. The constant crossbreed either in terms of beats, rhythms or instrumentation between different cultures globally especially in music attests to the representation that Erlmann alludes to.

The above is important towards understanding the interconnectedness between music from Africa and other parts of the world. This stems from the understanding that a process of hybridisation has taken place over the years, thus precipitating a need to redefine our musics. But one critic warns readers of the dangers of consummating this hybridisation wholesomely. Stephanie Newell, writing on popular literature in West Africa, warns critics against misusing the 'globalisation theory'. Newell dismisses the 'globalisation theorists' who tend to focus on the effects of western popular culture as it permeates the postcolonial societies. These theorists present 'local audiences in postcolonial states as the passive consumers of a drug-like alien culture, slowly becoming 'committed' to mass-produced western forms' (2000:3). By drawing these binaries, popular culture is seen as mimicry, flowing only from the affluent North to the impoverished South. What this research takes into consideration, however, is that the musicians and the audience are 'continually regenerating popular narratives, beats and rhythms creating models from the borrowed element and localising the foreign to such an extent that it cannot easily be placed in a separate sphere' (Newell, 2000:4)[23].

Coplan (1982:118) argues that in the case of African popular music, there is the blending of various western traditions into the structure of urban-based African culture patterns. He adds, 'once the outlines of a new model are in place, culture-contact becomes a double process in which African elements are re-interpreted in adopted western terms as well as western elements in African ones'.

With the culture-contact, new trends in African musics emerge. A lot of music in Africa in the late 90s is almost parallel to the rap and hip-hop culture in the western world especially America. Kwaito in South Africa is a case in point, as a music that maintains the South African touch but fits in the global hip-hop culture.[24] Waterman (1990:231) captures the cultural interaction quite aptly in his seminal work on *Juju* music in Nigeria. He propounds that while music talks about the daily experiences and expresses personal feelings, 'it may be used to refer to a domain of emergent trends in global systems of political economy which are complexly registered in language, emotions and the imagination'.

This argument is that music has to be extended to new uses beyond the musical contexts with which it had been associated before. Musicians are employing the beat, the rhythm and the lyrics to express, to mediate and often symbolically to resolve commonly held preoccupations about money, religion, marriage, gender and other issues. The songs 'open up symbolic spaces for the expression of these complex, ideologically mediated attitudes and opinions'. (Newell, 2000:8).

Musicians like Ndarlin' P in the 1990s produced Gĩkũyũ songs which leaned heavily on the hip-hop style. This research, though making mention of other forms in Gĩkũyũ music, restricts itself to the *benga* beat of musicians who have already made a name over the years to their audience. Such include Joseph Kamaru, Joseph Kariuki, Queen Jane, Albert Gacheru and *Mũgithi* artists.

Due to the multi-ethnic and cultural diversity in Kenya, it is always difficult to talk of a single, identifiable national music. Kenya has over 42 different communities, each with disparate cultures. But the poor performance of the music and musicians in the local and global context can be attributed to motley of other factors.

In the 1990s, the Kenyan media was subject to strict and insidious government censorship, and exploited the musicians' economic gains by restricting their access to financial reward and professional status. John Kariuki[25] argues that political interference in Kenya stood in the way of the musicians, especially those trying to promote the local languages. For example, Kariuki continues, 'in the year 2000, the Communication Commission of Kenya sought to bar private stations from broadcasting in vernacular languages so as to 'promote national building'. This meant that stations like Kameme FM, then, which broadcasts in Gĩkũyũ, would have been closed[26].

Ted Josiah, a leading music producer in Kenya agrees that, 'vernacular stations are actually a means of promoting appreciation of the country's cultural diversity. We should have more of them playing music in various Kenyan languages instead of suppressing them. We need to encourage the evolution of a truly multi-lingual culture in Kenya'.[27]

Another great obstacle in the Kenyan music scene has been the problem of piracy. Despite immense efforts by the Music Copyright Society in Kenya, the vice goes on unabated. May and Stapleton (1989), writing on this problem, attributed the proliferation of piracy partly to the dwindling economy, where the breadwinners simply don't have the cash for luxuries, and partly because the local recording companies until recently had no interest in local musicians. The existence of vernacular stations in the late 1990s and 2000 has ameliorated the situation to some extent. On the other hand, piracy can as well be seen as a necessary evil for it benefits the musicians by popularising their music.

In the last twenty years, the radio and the Compact Disc players are two forms of mass media, which have opened the floodgates to a literal invasion of imported musical forms, and led to the relegation of Kenyan popular music, especially in urban areas to near oblivion in the years under review. In recent years, however, local artists have embraced the new technologies and appropriated them to their advantage. The proliferation of high technology recording studios alongside youth-oriented radio stations like Kiss FM, Y FM, Ghetto FM etc. have given the local musician a major boost.

A study of Gĩkũyũ music in Kenya, therefore, has to incorporate all these dynamics, ranging from the context of performance, production and distribution, to the kind of themes and genres used, and the disparate styles of the music. Broadly, this encapsulates the idea of the 'politics of everyday life in the popular music'.

Music as text[28]

Unlike the approach taken by most musicologists and ethnomusicologists, the underlying principle in this research project is that music can be studied as a text. Text, as Hanks (1989:95) argues, can be taken to designate any configuration of signs that is coherently interpretable by some community of users. Music in this context fits aptly. As he argues, therefore, 'a narrative, a poem ...a piece of music display specific features of format; a beginning, middle, ending; compositional units such as episodes, scenes, sections, turns and stanzas; and genre categories, depending on the case at hand'. Text also entails the oral performance.

Agawu's (2001:8) argument is quite instrumental in this research. He clearly acknowledges that contemporary African music can be studied as a text. Agawu notes that in so far as they constitute complex messages rooted in specific cultural practices, the varieties of African music known to us today may be designated as a text. He adds that 'while performing practice and audience participation vary according to genre, the activity of meaning construction remains essential to all participants'.

Euba (2001:121) amplifies the same point and argues for the text setting in African compositions. Drawing his analysis from traditional music, he asserts;

> If traditional music is so highly text-oriented, it is reasonable to conclude that texts are crucial to the understanding of music in African societies. Modern composers who seek to communicate with African audiences are therefore well advised to consider texts as one of their means of doing so.

In line with the argument, this conviction remains that music of any kind is an important organ in articulating the daily upheavals as well as successes in a society, and hence demands ample investigation and appreciation. A brief look into the historical background of the Kenyan music above has amplified and justified reasons for this particular study.

The phrase 'politics of everyday life' is used in this context to refer to the 'actualities of individual interaction within the society' as Terence Ranger (1991:149) aptly puts it, and it is in no way private (in this way, the Gĩkũyũ) experiences as opposed to public (the larger Kenyan context), or microcosmic as opposed to macrocosmic. It is an appreciation of complex pluralities of cultural production practice and ideas, that is, music, rather than artificially isolating one ethnic community.

In power relations, politics doesn't necessarily remain a relationship between the ruler and the ruled only. Every other facet of our lives derives or has a bearing towards the politics of the day. Popular culture in Scott's (1990:37-8) words provides a "hidden transcript" in which is written 'the anger and reciprocal aggression denied by the presence of domination'. This hidden transcript, he argues, is found in rumours, folktales, gossip, jokes, songs, rituals, codes, and euphemism (1990:19).

Therefore, politics should not be seen as simply occurring through coercion, consciousness or formal political mechanisms, but in 'informal processes of socialisation. Domination, therefore, can also be 'resisted through informal means, including cultural practices like music' (Balliger, 1999:68-9). Thus music does not reside in music texts themselves but in their articulation with society. The articulation then encapsulates what this research appropriates as the politics of everyday life.

The interaction between popular culture and politics, or in finer terms between music and society involves a struggle over subject-producing practices which gain meaning in specific contents and moments, rhythms, sounds, and collective spaces may affirm ways of being and produce embodiment in opposition to dominant society. Popular culture then becomes, not always a site of resistance, but also of asserting authority, depending on the moment of production and the meaning attached to the song.

Storey, (1996:4) notes:

> Meaning is ... a social production; the world has to be made to mean. A text or practice or event is not the issuing source of meaning, but a site where the articulation of meaning – variable meaning(s) – can take place... Because different meanings can be ascribed to the same text or practice or event, meaning is always a potential site of conflict ... it is a terrain of incorporation and resistance; one of the sites where hegemony is to be won or lost.

With musical lyrics being subjected to various meanings, music then goes beyond simply beats and rhythm. This study deliberately sees music as a social construct, social text that captures and articulates the day-to-day experiences of the society. Bebey's (1974:3) argument that African music is not only a combination of sounds in a manner pleasing to the ear, is important in this research. The aim of music, as Bebey argues, is to 'simply express life in all of its aspects through the medium of sound.'[29]

Popular music as an aspect of popular culture

This study also looks at the notions of the popular to contextualise music in relation to day-to-day experiences. Although most contemporary musicians have indulged in music as a means of livelihood, this research is also aware of the fact that people tend to become musicians not so much from personal vocations as from a need to fulfil a social obligation.[30]

Bender (1991: xvi) suggests that what is involved in calling a type of music popular is that the music has to be ready to get to the common people. Bender argues that 'for the music to become something that is part of the culture, the people need technical means and certain social contexts to be in place as a matter of development before music moves away from its elite form. At that point, the society itself has become something else'.

The music analysed here deals with all sorts of problems, achievements and failures in a daily experience. As Coplan (1982:116) notes, 'popular music ... provides a multiplicity of meanings accommodating a range of manipulation, interpretation and choice, and supplies a measure of solidarity in an environment characterised by social insecurity, dislocation and differentiation'.

Music like other forms of art also creates symbolic structures within which a certain form of integration takes place. Musicians, in their lyrics, address issues that appear commonsensical. They mobilise a variety of methods to name and describe the world in an idiom and symbolism, which is familiar and understandable. This 'elicits a "consensus" or agreement with the narrative as "natural" and "reasonable" '(Gecau: 2002:50). The audiences' perceive this as reconfirming the meanings they have made out of their daily activities. Coplan's argument above becomes crucial in the interrogation of the kinds of identities that are constructed in the process of this search of solidarity in preceding chapters.

Music, therefore, expresses and symbolises processes, like disillusionment, anxieties and fears amongst other things. Chernoff (1979:32) asserts that music remains somewhat beyond our daily lives, having little direct relationship to what we are doing most of the time'. Though dealing with day-to-day problems, music is not just a simple mechanical reflection of reality.

In almost similar terms, Blacking supports the argument when he suggests that 'ordinary daily experience takes place in a world of actual time. The essential quality of music is its power to create another world of virtual time' (1995:225). Basically, therefore, music here provides a different take and handle on reality and in the same vein expressing optimism and hope in times of anguish and disenchantment. This is not always the case, though. The tone and the message in other instances is tragic and saddening.

Bebey's statement indicates this very precisely in his analysis of music in Africa. He asserts ... 'however transcendent the substance of African music(s) may be, it is always expressed at a human level... The celestial music that is raised to the glory of the gods [especially in traditional music] has its roots in the terrestrial realities of daily life' (1974:132). This emphasises the above argument on virtual realities in music as put across by Blacking. And as Erlmann (1999:6) notes:

> Unlike any other aspect of mass culture, music organises social interaction in ways that are no longer determined by the primacy of locally situated practice and collectively maintained memory ... instead; music becomes a medium that mediates, as it were, mediation. In other words, music in global culture, by a dint of a number of significant shifts in the production, circulation and consumption of musical sounds, functions as an interactive social context, a conduit for other forms of interaction, other socially mediated forms of appropriation of the world'

The strand of thought pursued in relation to the above is that music should not in any way be perceived or treated as a separate reality though, but as a component of the daily lives and experiences. Unlike movies, music does not express a form of mechanised form of living. Music becomes what Gilroy (1999:9) calls 'a privileged signifier for an obstinate and consistent commitment to the ideas of a better future'[31]. Music is, thus, both a species of culture pattern and a mode of human action in and upon the world.

McQuail (1993:36) defines popular culture as that whose characteristics would be of 'spontaneous origination and persistence in social life under very varied forms, e.g. language, dress, music, custom and so forth'. There is no reason to doubt that living societies continue to produce much popular culture from the variety of forms. This research imperative is mostly on popular music, but instances where the different forms of popular culture interact will be dealt with. Though of 'spontaneous origination', most of these forms of popular culture point towards the interaction between society and its people in the day-to-day realities of life.

For example, The *Mũthĩrĩgũ* song genre among the Gĩkũyũ community in the 1920s emerged due to political upheavals in Kenya. It was an 'expression of protest against the colonial power's suppression of African traditional values' (Muhoro: 1997:102). The proponents of *Mũthĩrĩgũ* protest songs emphasised the female genital mutilation rite of passage as a means of maintaining Gĩkũyũ culture. Presently, the emergence of the *Mũgithi* performance in the late 1990s and the reasons behind its origins clearly denote the fact that despite the spontaneity, the politics of the day greatly contributed to its widespread appeal especially in urban centres. This is dealt with in preceding chapters.

Whereas this research will not be inundated with the diverse definitions around the notion of the popular and popular culture, a working definition may suffice. In situations where the interface of popular culture and politics is investigated, then the idea of the popular is seen as a political moral category: 'the definition of the popular being that which functions in the interests of the masses (the farmers, workers, unemployed) by opening up their eyes to their own objective, historical situation, the actual conditions of their existence and thus enabling them to empower themselves' (Barber, 1997:5). Masses are not always unaware of their predicaments. Popular culture just accentuates their feeling of hopelessness, but at the same time coalescing their misery as an arsenal against assumed prejudices. Street (1997:10) reflecting on the interconnectedness between popular culture and politics agrees that:

> Popular culture's ability to produce and articulate feelings can become the basis of an identity, and that identity can be the source of political thought and action.

It is in trying to articulate emotions that popular culture links us to the outside world. The popular music investigated in this research does not just reflect emotions, but plays out 'everyday moral dilemmas, posing questions and suggesting answers to our worries, about what we should do' (Street, 1997:9)

There is a prudent deliberation in this research not to view these cultural expressions as *only* mirrors of a society or a nation. According to Fabian, (1978:23) culture does not only mirror, it also symbolizes and thus always have a sign-function. More than that, any living culture must be viewed as a communicative process in which a society, not only expresses, but also generates and forms its worldview. But more importantly, as a vehicle through which people seek to integrate their lives particularly in dislocating moments such as the post-1990 years in Kenya. At the same time, however, the research will look into ways in which Gĩkũyũ popular music wills new cultural processes into being.

Human experiences are grounded in cultural activities, which are understood and given meanings through particular languages and symbol systems. These are in turn constituted within particular social circumstances and subject to different types of political regulation.

The definition of popular culture in this research is also modelled along Karin Barber's argument on African art. It is an appreciation of the music as a form of entertainment 'usually talking about matters of deep interest and concern to the people who produce and consume them (Barber, 1997:2). She acknowledges that whereas the music is not explicitly committed art, it is an art which speaks to people about the conditions of their existence. Notes Bender (1991:131):

> The texts [music] deal with all possible themes, anything that affects people on the streets. They are social commentaries and moral considerations; unemployment, the rent, alcohol, prostitution and laziness [are] taken up as subjects. Addressing everyday problems should also be seen as a continuation of the traditional function of music.

Worth noting from the above quote is that distinct differences are noticeably gleaned between traditional music and popular music which forms the mainstay of this research. It is true that unlike the traditional musician, contemporary musicians much as being commentators of the politics of daily life also think of their music means of livelihood. Whether they live up to these expectations or not is a debate I am going to discuss later in the study, together with the politics of production, distribution and marketing in contemporary Kenya.

The above definitions of popular culture are crucial in this research. Most songs deal with politics though not explicitly. One artist, Queen Jane's song, *'Hawkers'* is quite illustrative. On the one hand, she decries the daily upheavals and struggles of a hawker along the streets of Nairobi. She portrays the hawker trying to eke out a living amid frustrations caused by the city council authorities. On the other hand, the song can be interpreted as a scathing attack on the government. It is not by choice that these people trade their wares on the streets. It is a pointer to the high levels of unemployment and a declining economy. The government has failed to live up to the expectations of the citizens. The musician likens the hawkers to the plight of Israelites in Egypt as recorded in the

Bible; which brings me to the issue of borrowing from other milieus, or simply put, intertextuality.

Allen (2000:174-175) explores the issue of intertextuality in the non-literary arts like film, paintings, symphonies, music and paintings and argues that 'they constantly talk to each other as well as talking to other arts' and disciplines if I may add. The argument foregrounds an earlier position of appreciating music as a text. Quoting Robert Hatten, Allen (ibid) comments on the manner in which a composer's 'competence in particular music styles and that same composer's strategic utilization of those styles in particular music pieces constitute "regulators of relevant intertextual relationship"'.

Intertextuality in Kenyan music as argued before in the study is not just on themes, styles but also on the rhythm and the beat. one is immediately reminded of many songs that have mixed both the western aspects and the traditional. Musically, Hardstone Ngunjiri's song, Ūhiki' (Wedding), as discussed earlier, is a clear rendition of Marvin Gaye's song Sexual Healing but it is done in Gĩkũyũ and addressing pertinent issues like bride price and dowry among the community.

Most studies on music are usually found in ethnomusicology. As AbiolaIrele (2001:1), argues, the view propounded by ethnomusicologists comes with its own limitations and discrepancies. Irele acknowledges that this approach to African music in ethnomusicology 'precludes any consideration of a possible connection between its [African music] heritage and other musical traditions around the world'. Studies in ethnomusicology presuppose a disparity between the non-western forms of musical practice and expressions and those that are taken to constitute the western musical tradition.

The consequence of this narrow approach, Irele argues is that African music is conditioned to a definition that authentic music in Africa is only the traditional music, which is only definable, by rhythm 'to the exclusion of other aspects that are constitutive of its syntax as a form of musical language (2001:2).' The intensity, richness and variety of the landscape in African music is always ignored in ethnomusicology.

Neither musicology is innocent of ignoring the social context of music and song performance. Shepherd (1991:190) argues that musicology fails not only to recognise the inherently social nature of music but, through that, fails as well to recognize the possible specifics of music as a social form. His contention (1991:164) is that the sounds of popular music are in some way connected to and of consequence for the people whose subjectivities and lives popular music affects them. He adds, 'Music as text ... can be thought of as an element of culture and thus susceptible to the scrutiny of various forms of cultural theory and of the linguistic theory that support them'. (1991:162)

Music can also be appreciated as a source of documentation about political, economic and social life. As Barber (1997:5) aptly puts it, this kind of text usually says only the things that people want to hear. But while it is true that people usually want to hear that justice will prevail and that the good will be rewarded, they do not apparently want to hear escapist fantasies. As she adds, if there is confraternity in suffering, then aspiration towards self-betterment life is another one that follows from it. This leads me to the discussion on popular music in the politics of everyday life.

While this study is on Gĩkũyũ music, this chapter has provided a broad overview of the growth of postcolonial Kenyan music. However, great emphasis is put on Gĩkũyũ music and its traditional antecedents, while at the same time locating the community in the larger terrain of Kenya. Music, in this research initiative is looked at as an aspect of popular culture as well as a text. These are issues the study addresses in the latter section of this chapter. Chapter Two is a representation of how popular music forms part of the everyday practice of the Gĩkũyũ community. It is a reflection on this music *vis-à-vis* the events that dominated the politics of the decade, from 1990 to 2000. Music from a number of prominent artists is put on the spotlight.

Paying particular attention to the interplay between music and politics, the theme of patriotism and its contested versions form the backbone of Chapter Three. Music is presented as a site for power contestation in Kenya drawing connections between praise and protest songs in both colonial and postcolonial Kenya.

The fourth chapter concerns itself with the music of Joseph Kamaru, the guru of Gĩkũyũ music. His music, which straddles the three ruling regimes of postcolonial Kenya alongside his response to major political events in the history of the country is analysed. Kamaru's skilful appropriation of the Gĩkũyũ traditions and customs in his music is also explored.

Chapters Five and Six delve into the politics and poetics of an emergent genre in Gĩkũyũ music, referred to as *Mũgithi*. This major concern here is the playing of identities. The interplay between the tradition and modern, urban and rural, secular and religious are discussed in the fifth chapter, while Chapter Six looks at ethnic and national identities' interface in postcolonial Kenya.

The conclusion is an overview of all the chapters and fleshes out the main arguments in this research project. The conclusion also considers possibilities for future research on popular music in Kenya.

Notes

[1] Though the period under study is between 1990 and 2000, it is worthwhile noting that themes discussed and analysed are not restricted to the decade since issues that musicians sang on and about in the 1990s are also prevalent in music of 2000 and beyond.

[2] Kenya has over 42 ethnic communities, which are categorized into three linguistic groups, Bantus the Nilotes, and Cushites. The communities include Luhya, Kisii, Kuria, Kikuyu, Kamba, Meru, Embu, Tharaka, Mbere, Mijikenda (Digo, Duruma, Rabai, Ribe, Kambe, Jibana, Chonyi, Giriama, Kauma), Taveta, Pokomo, Taita, Iteso, Turkana, Nandi, Kipsigis, Elgeyo, Sabaot, Marakwet, Tugen, Terik, Pokot, Somali, Rendille, Galla, Borana/Boran, Gabbra, Orma, Sakuye and Swahili.

[3] According to the CIA World Factbook, these are the percentages of the major ethnic groups in Kenya: Gĩkũyũ 22%, Luhya 14%, Luo 13%, Kalenjin 12%, Kamba 11%, Kisii 6%, Meru 6%, other African 15%, non-African (Asian, European, and Arab) 1%. https://www.cia.gov/library/publications/the-world-factbook/geos/ke.html. In the 2009 Kenyan government census, the Gĩkũyũ accounted for 6.6 million of the total population of 38.6 million people.
http://www.knbs.or.ke/docs/PresentationbyMinisterforPlanningrevised.pdf

[4] Cristiana Pugliese, *Author, Publisher and Gĩkũyũ Nationalist: The Life and Writings of Gakaara wa Wanjau*. Bayreuth: E. Breitinger, 1995, p. 89.

[5] Nairobi was originally the name given to the marsh on which the city stands, by the Maasai, who were known to the Gĩkũyũ as *Ũkabi*. See Muriuki, (1974: 87). The Maasai called the place *Enkare Nairobi* or place of cold water. Diana Kasyoka. Daily Nation, 23 May 2005.

[6] In recent years, some of these stations are broadcasting nationwide. Kameme FM and Inooro FM, for instance are also accessible to the Gīkūyū in the Diaspora via the Internet onhttp://www.kameme.co.ke and www.inoorofm.co.ke. Several other vernacular stations from the different communities have proliferated as well, e.g. Ramogi FM which broadcasts in Dholuo, Mulembe FM for the Luhya, etc.

[7] Most Gīkūyū songs in this study fall in what is referred to as the *benga* beat. In Kenya, the beat is the domain and invention of the Luo community though there is a clear link to a Congolese beat which is quite similar. What is called Kikuyu *benga* is a variation of the Luo *benga* beat.

[8] Murang'a is a town in central Kenya, inhabited mainly by the Gīkūyū community. Immediately after independence, most Gīkūyū people from Murang'a established business premises along River Road. Presently, most recording studios are found along and around this street.

[9]Kimani Njogu (1997) also argues that popular culture transcends ethnic, geographical and national boundaries because it can be disseminated by electronic and print media by roving performers beyond the boundaries of its place of creation.

[10] This study however relies mostly on the stylistic choices embedded in the lyrics.

[11] Most musicians however outgrew the negative attitude attributed to the music profession and rose to become great artists in later years. D.O Misiani greatest hits were especially in the 80s and 90s while Albert Gacheru is quite famous among the Gīkūyū due to his songs in the 1990s.

[12] Mimbi, according to the myth of origin of the Gīkūyū people is the mother of the community. The Gīkūyū people invoke the name of their mythical ancestors when the community feels threatened.

[13] Dedan Kīmathi was the leader of the Mau Mau movement which was crucial in the attainment of Kenya's independence from the British in 1963. Kīmathi represents the ideals and principles that independence was supposed to achieve for the young Kenyan nation.

[14] Wanjiku Mukabi Kabira and Karega wa Mutahi. *Gīkūyū Oral Literature*. East African Educational Publishers. Nairobi. 1988, pp 18-26.

[15] *Mwomboko* is a song genre derived from *Mūthīrīgū*, coastal dances and some Luhya and Luo folk songs. 'It has a strong touch of the Scottish dance in its choreography' (Muhoro, 1997: 103). The accordion is a significant instrumental accompaniment. *Mwomboko* men and women dance in pairs. Men press their partners to their chests, and occasionally spin them around. It is performed with an accordion and iron cymbals

[16] Recent research of the music of the Gĩkũyũ people shows that the country music genre has had immense influence on the musicians. The dress style as well as the lyrics echo some of the key characteristics of Western country musicians like Jimmy Rodgers. See Mutonya et al., *Retracing Kikuyu Music*, 2010. p. 10.

[17] Chris Stapleton and Chris May. *African All Stars: The Pop Music of a Continent.* London: Grafton, 1989, p226. They cite musicians like Franco, Sam Mangwana and Tabu Ley, who built up huge followings in East Africa, generally setting a precedent for musicians like Mzee Makassy and Samba Mapangala who settled permanently in the area.

[18] Most pre-colonial societies in Kenya boast of a strong tradition of stringed instruments, but more specifically, the communities from western Kenya who were celebrated for their skill with harps and lyres; the Luo had Nyatiti, Orutu and the Luhya had Litungu which brought out rhythms and dances like *bodi*, *sukuma* and *umotibi*. See Stapleton and May (1989:227).

[19] Kwela is a happy, often pennywhistle based, street music from southern Africa with jazzy underpinnings. It evolved from the *marabi* sound and brought South African music to international prominence in the 1950s. http://en.wikipedia.org/wiki/Kwela.

[20] Daniel Owino Misiani is credited for pushing the Luo dance rhythms into acoustic guitar.

[21] Swahili language is widely spoken in East and Central Africa. In Tanzania, it is the official language, while any Kenyan who has gone through the secondary schooling, studies the language. In the Democratic Republic of Congo it is mostly spoken in the eastern region. Ugandans, Rwandans, Burundians and Zambians bordering Tanzania too speak the language.

[22] Lingala is spoken in Democratic Republic of Congo, but music from this country is widespread across the region even where the audience does not speak nor understand the language.

[23] It should be noted that popular culture is essentially free, dynamic and ever changing. It always resists containment and challenges and collapses the binaries between traditional and modern, foreign and indigenous, official and unofficial. Kimani Njogu (1997) propounds the point that popular culture is localized, appropriated and redefined through being assigned new meanings and modes of representation.

[24] Simon Stephens (2000:256) traces the emergence of *Kwaito* as an evolution of music known as 'bubblegum', or South African disco 'with elements of American hip-hop, European house music and other international sounds'. The music maintains a distinct

South African identity by the use of *tsotsitaal*, a township slang that combines various South African languages.

[25] Kariuki, John. "Forget your Language and Lose your Culture" in *The East African*, 3rd March 2002.

[26] The situation has since improved with a number of vernacular stations in various languages licensed and fully operational.

[27] Kariuki., *Op.cit*

[28] It should be made clear at this juncture that in the scope of this research, what I call text specifically is the lyrics of the songs. This emanates from the understanding that even jazz or instrumental music is a text of its own, though devoid of words.

[29] Francis Bebey: *African Music: A People's Art*. (London: Harrap, 1974), p. 3. Bebey further argues that music is an integral part of African life from the cradle to the grave and that African music covers the widest possible range of expression, including spoken language and all manner of natural sounds (p 17).

[30] Gicingiri wa Ndigirigi, in an article in the Gĩkũyũ Journal *Mũtiiri* lauds Joseph Kamaru, a prominent Gĩkũyũ musician, as a 'public teacher'. This rhymes well with Chinua Achebe's assertion of ' The Novelist as the Teacher' in *Hopes and Impediments. Selected Essays 1965-1987*. (London: Heinemann, 1988)

[31] Paul Gilroy, *The Black Atlantic: Modernity and Double Consciousness*, quoted in Erlmann Veit's, *Music, Modernity and the Global Imagination*. (New York and Oxford: Oxford University Press, 1999: 9)

CHAPTER TWO

The Politics of Everyday Life in Select Gĩkũyũ Popular Music (1990-2000)

...[W]e must contend with the fact that even under the most oppressive of conditions, people are always trying and struggling to maintain a semblance of normal social order. They will attempt to apply tradition and custom to manage their day-to-day family problems: they will resort to socially acquired behaviour pattern to eke out a means of subsistence. They apply systems of values that they know. Often those values will undergo changes under certain pressing conditions. The transformation of those values constitutes the essential drama in the lives of ordinary people (Njabulo Ndebele, 1991:53).

This chapter is a presentation on how popular music of the Gĩkũyũ community in Kenya has been experienced across the immediate surfaces of everyday life, especially in the decade under review, 1990-2000. It is, therefore, an investigation into how music and musicians form an integral part in the daily lives of its people. Touching on almost all aspects of life, the music comments and responds to issues that affect the listeners, but in way that the lyrics resonate with the listeners' daily experiences. By drawing on select artistes from the Gĩkũyũ community in Kenya[1], this chapter examines how these musicians contextualize their work of art in everyday life by appropriating or using the local repertoire, representative of their societies. Music then becomes a symbolic representation of day-to-day struggles.

In the context of this study, the 'politics of everyday' refers to the many dimensions of social interaction, 'from the mediating role of institutions, to the expression of ideals, to the relationship between interests and identities' (Street, 1997:42). Politics, as Street further argues, extends beyond the formal boundaries of the constitution and the political processes, as they are conventionally understood. It extends to the ways in which people see themselves and those around them.

Popular music has been an expressive form in which the politics of everyday life has been played out and performed. The focus on popular music is based on the understanding that music has a 'captive audience out there situated in locales outside the regulated zones of the leadership' (Nyairo and Ogude, 2003:384). Herein lies the power of the music in articulating the tribulations, hopes, desires, anxieties and dreams of the citizenry. In this way, this music can be seen as a 'platform for debate and action against the elite's dominant ideology' (Chirambo, 2002:103).

This resistance dimension is propagated by Chambers (1985:209), as he characterises popular music as an 'important counter-space in our daily lives which can escape from, or challenge various socially enforced routines and categories'.

In this vein, however, it is important to note that this music should not just be seen from this functional perspective, for this would deny musicians their creative abilities. But it is the musicians' stance on the ordinary in the daily life of the people that this chapter concerns itself with. Bodil Frederiksen's[2] take on the ordinary is quite illuminating. While discussing the popular arts in East Africa, he argues that for urban Africans, an ordinary, comfortable everyday life free of misery and harassment is the adventure. He adds that the opposite is the norm. The multiple themes expressed in the songs analysed in the chapter, exemplifies a quest for a better life, an 'ordinary life' to appropriate Frederiksen's phrase. But they also touch on issues that affect their day-to-day experiences.

A cursory glance at some of the titles of the songs reviewed best illustrates this. Themes include love relationships, for instance, Queen Jane's *Nĩtwatiganire* (we are already divorced), Peter Kigia's *Reke Tũtigane* (Let us divorce) or Joseph Kariuki's *Nyagũthiĩ*, (a female Gĩkũyũ's name); class and social differences, e.g., Jane's *Hawkers*, or Kigia's *Coro wa Athĩni* (The trumpet of the poor), and *Ciana cia Athĩni* (Children of the wretched); politics in Albert Gacheru's *Gatiba nĩ Ĩcenjio* (Change the constitution) or Kigia's *Bũrũri wa Gĩkũyũ* (The Gĩkũyũ Nation).

Many popular [arts] from Kenya, Tanzania and Nigeria, Frederiksen (2002:95) argues, are best seen as realistic fantasies, meticulously describing the lives of the fabulously rich. Or the lives of the not so rich in terms of their efforts to grab and enjoy a modern lifestyle, closely associated with regular work and ability to afford school fees:

> The ordinary is the utopia. But in a dynamic situation, the ordinary has to be imagined and constructed. In this creative process, popular arts and popular culture more broadly play a key role. In areas of popular culture, issues central to the everyday life of the majority of population are being articulated and debated, and new modes of life are made visible, audible, [and] thinkable.

In a statement echoing the same, (Fabian 1990:19) argues that the kind of performances we find in popular culture have become, for the people involved more than ever, ways to 'preserve some respect in the face of constant humiliation and to set the wealth of artistic creativity against an environment of utter poverty. All this is not to be dismissed off-hand as escape from reality. It is realistic praxis under the concrete political and economic conditions that reign'.

This study is situated in the post-1990 years – rightly depicted as an age of major sociopolitical transformations and upheavals, of the momentous collapse of the Cold-War order, which also ushered in the struggles to create a 'new' order. The research fills an important gap by adeptly using popular music as a form of political oppression and the musician as a critical social player to understand the intricacies of Kenya's turbulent politics in the crucial 1990s and after.

An exposé of the Kenya in the 1990s below provides a background in which the music under review proliferated. The early 1990s in most of Africa saw the re-emergence of multi-party politics, but which was met by intense resistance from the ruling regimes. In Kenya, the 1982 constitutional amendment had made Kenya a *de jure* one-party state, and the government of Daniel arap Moi intensified its crackdown on individuals who were not toeing the official line. In the 1990s, Moi also became increasingly suspicious of even close political allies. In the environment of this mistrust, Moi dealt ruthlessly with real or imagined enemies; fellow politicians, academics, lawyers, church leaders, musicians, farmers, university students etc. This background created a situation in the country in which 'the government was afraid of its citizens and the citizens were afraid of their government. There was a mutual fear of the ruler and the ruled; a condition that was dubbed *paramoia*'

(Kariuki, 1996:70), a pun on the president's name. While the 1980s in Kenya were characterized by silences and fear, as well as the zenith of the dictatorial regime of Moi, the 1990s witnessed heightened political electricity in the clamor for the multi-party democracy, a dream that was actualized in 1991, but which did not come with a change of regime. This, therefore, meant that the excesses of the one party rule never diminished overnight. In fact, the more the Kenyans criticized the ruling regime, the stricter the government became intolerant to what it referred to as dissent, but what was in fact a proliferation of the opposition activity.

With the re-introduction of multi-party democracy in the early 1990s[3] Kenyans also looked forward to competitive politics, which would usher in new patterns of leadership and hence lessen the general suffering. In their minds, an ambience of hope that could ossify problems into solutions was within reach. But this was never to be. Social and political malaise continued unabated.

However, in the country, frustrations and disenchantment carried on, especially over the lack of the much-anticipated change. The 'failure of the opposition parties to remove the Moi regime at the last election (1992) fostered a situation in which ordinary people [were] beginning to ask whether genuine changes can be brought about through the ballot box' (Ajulu, 1995:229). However, the major undoing of the opposition parties in Kenya then was the fact that most of these parties 'crystallized mostly on the basis of ethnic and regional interests, rather than common ideology and political principles', (Osamba, 2001:37). This, coupled with disunity among these parties meant that the stranglehold under Daniel Moi and his KANU[4] party was not broken.

The continued rule under Daniel Moi also meant a continuum of the travesties of justice, economic mismanagement, tribalism, corruption and human rights abuse that had characterised the regime since 1978 when Moi took over the helms of leadership. Upon assuming power, Moi had promised reforms in all sectors. However, rather than provide reforms, 'his anti-corruption drive was in fact a tool against the Kikuyu elite who had accumulated power and wealth during the Kenyatta era' (Kariuki, 1996:74). This strategy was, however, resented because it was reminiscent of Kenyatta's antics between 1963 till his death in 1978 when most 'non-Kikuyus were marginalized in the country's political economy' (Kariuki, 1996:77). To consolidate his power in later years,

Moi engineered a remake of Kenyatta's 'multi-ethnic elite alliance in a way that seriously diminished the economic and political power of the Kikuyu faction' (Berman, Eyo and Kymlicka, 2004:10). Notes Adar and Munyae (2001)

> To bolster his grip on power, Moi embarked on the gradual Kalenjinization of the public and private sectors from the 1980s. Moi is a Tugen, one of the smaller Kalenjin ethnic groups. He began to 'de-Kikuyunize' the civil service and state-owned enterprises previously dominated by the Kikuyu ethnic group during Kenyatta's regime.

A sentiment shared by Hempstone (1997:39).

> ... [Moi] enlisted and promoted his tribesmen in disproportionate numbers in the army and civil service. Promotion in both depended, not on competence but on unquestioning loyalty and subservience to the accidental Big Man, from whom all power, privilege and wealth derive.

Politicised tribalism, in Kenya, has continued egregiously under different regimes since independence. As argued later, this aspect is partly a colonial legacy, where colonialists categorised their subjects in relation to their ethnic backgrounds to prevent some form of unity. Post-independence governments have, however, perfected the art in attempt to hold on to power. As Odhiambo (2002:171-2) shows, ethnicity in Kenya permeates the lives of ordinary Kenyans who 'talk and think about it as the regular experience of their everyday lives, in its many enabling capacities, its incapacitating impediments on the hopes of individuals and the blocking of opportunities for whole communities'. It is through the understanding of the patron-client relationships that define Kenyan politics, as Schatzberg (1988:22) rightly argues that 'ethnicities may arise in opposition to the state specifically when a group feels excluded from the benefits the state has to offer and thus relatively disadvantaged'.

The ethnic allocation of offices through quotas or assignment of particular positions simply formalized the prevailing practices of patronage in Kenyan politics, both under Kenyatta and Moi. The president's power in Kenya currently is enhanced by a system of patronage and corruption. The fact that the president is in charge of distributing state largesse makes people 'more conscious of their specific links to those with power, wealth and influence' Schatzberg (1988:14). The culture and politics of patron-client relationship and enhancement of ethnicities in Kenya thus persists through and through.

The above clearly informed the politics of the 1990s despite the country having adopted a multi-party democracy. The politics of Kenya in the 1990s were clearly of a Machiavellian nature where, 'situations were manipulated to derive the maximum advantage to those in power', (Bakari, 2002:1). The ruling party was seen more as a tool of self-enrichment and self-aggrandizement by both party politicians and the general public at large. The ruling regime could not at any point brook any dissent. Suppression of the freedom of press, assembly, association, expression and movement and other fundamental rights was applied on the press, civil society, the clergy, lawyers, academics and ordinary people whose actions were seen as bordering subversion. For example, in 1991, 'Moi banned the production of George Orwell's play, *Animal Farm.* He also banned Ngugi wa Thiong'o's play *Ngaahika Ndeenda* (I Will Marry When I Want), considered by the regime to be subversive because it attacks post-independence African dictators' (Adar and Munyae, 2001:7).

The tradition of murder and assassination went on unabated. A number of charismatic politicians lost their lives through political assassination or perceived assassination. During both Kenyatta and Moi's regimes, prominent leaders like Pio Gama Pinto, Tom Mboya and J.M Kariuki were assassinated while Ronald Ngala, Robert Ouko and Bishop Muge died under mysterious circumstances but with fingers pointing to the respective government's involvement. The Machiavellian nature ensured that politicians who came in the way of particular interests were forced to toe the line through persuasion, bribing, intimidation and resort to physical elimination if the other methods failed. Moi also made detention without trial and torture so common that in 1989 he explained it thus; 'Of course we torture people. But we don't torture everybody. We torture the ringleaders of Mwakenya[5]; otherwise how can we find information from them'. (Munene, 2004:9). Such were measures that Moi undertook to ensure minimal political competition, and hold onto power unchallenged.

The public suffered immensely in the 1990s owing to mismanagement of the country's economy, tribal clashes, corruption and looting of the national treasury by those holding power.

The disillusionment and dislocation of Kenyans in the 1990s was founded on unanswered questions of why bankrupting the public treasury, mass insecurity, ethnic discrimination, the rise of looting, widespread hopelessness and the economic meltdown has not been arrested by a multi-party democracy which Kenyans hoped that it could evolve a more accountable government and manage transitions by shopping among competing alternatives.

In terms of the state of the economy, the decade witnessed the plummeting of the Kenyan economy; from the mounting inflation, foreign debt, declining world market prices for principal export products such as coffee and tea and a decrease in foreign investment and tourism revenues. All these impacted heavily on the ordinary person in Kenya; given the fact the country's population is largely agrarian. By 1992, real economic growth had fallen to near zero. As Haugerud (1995:34) asserts, growth of real GDP was 2.5 % in 1991. In 1992, the agriculture sector declined by 4.2 %. The rate of inflation increased from 19.6% in 1991 to 27.5% in 1992'. As argued above, this had a direct impact on the ordinary Kenyan and fuelled discontent against the government and had a direct impact.

In the 1990s too, corruption had become a major problem hindering economic growth and poisoning every other facet of the nation. The structurally flawed Kenyan economy left the rural poor – the majority of the people – particularly disadvantaged. Hempstone (1997:33), comments on the state of affairs in the 1990s:

> The economy was visibly sagging and its society on the verge of becoming dysfunctional, with an appalling crime rate, and there was much political discontent. The government was in no mood to tolerate dissent always equated with subversion in Africa, or even to address the problem.

The above fits in Bayart's (1993:60) argument that in Africa, 'the state is a major manufacturer of inequality. The 'development' it boastfully claims to promote and in whose name it attempts to ban political competition and social protest, plays a part in this process'.

The politics of ethnic hate re-emerged in the 1990s culminating into the infamous tribal clashes of 1991-1998. The impact of this hate has been the split of the nation into almost mutually exclusive ethnic blocs threatening and fearing each other.[6] Hitherto, the history of Kenya, however, has been founded on different ethnic nationalisms and the relation between them mostly defined by the politics of the day. In postcolonial Kenya, the ethnic background of the president has a large influence on how the different communities interact. Pointing to the symbiotic relationship between nationalism and ethnicity, Appadurai (1993:413) argues that the two 'feed each other, as nationalists construct ethnic categories that in turn drive others to construct counter ethnicities, and then in times of political crisis, these others demand counter states based on newfound counter nationalisms. For every nationalism that appears to be naturally destined, there is another that is a reactive by-product'.

Albert Gacheri's song, *Ndĩ Mũkenya* (I am a Kenyan) addresses the issue of tribalism in Kenya, but he urges his listeners to shun animosity amongst the different communities living in Kenya:

Ũndũ wa mbere andũ a Kenya - First thing Kenyans,
Mwambe mũnine ũkabira - let us stamp out tribalism
O mũndũ amenye nĩ Mũkenya -Everyone should know s/he is a Kenyan
Ndũrĩrĩ no ta Gĩkũyũ - Other tribes are just like the Gĩkũyũ
Ningĩ Akenya mũmenye biũ - Again, Kenyans, you should know
To thiomi ciki itiganaga - Though we speak different languages,
Bũrũri ũkoragwo hamwe - the nation is one.

However, although the nature of politics of Kenya is strongly local and ethnic, there is paradoxically a bright side to this. This ethnic nature can be seen a democratic boon in that it 'creates an important check against the centralization of power under an authoritarian leader' (Bellamy, 2004:62). The authoritarian leader that Moi was could never completely control or channel grassroots political energy, because leaders or members of parliament are elected directly by the voters and thus largely responsible to them. Thus, at the local level, Kenyans could still put pressure on their local leaders on issues that had a national bearing. Therefore, in this case, it was still possible, despite the government's intolerance to opposition, that there were still cells of opposition at the grassroots level and this mostly was represented by popular musicians, especially those singing in vernacular languages, whose messages reverberated with the experiences of the citizens on the ground.

The political and social displeasure manifested itself in increasing domestic violence, alcoholism and growing cynicism, notes Kituyi (2000). But in the same vein, several popular art forms also emerged. Barber (1987:4) notes that in times of rapid social change, the art forms 'with their exceptional mobility (whether through technology such as the radio, record and cassette tape, or through physical transportation from place to place by travelling performing groups) will play a crucial role in formulating new ways of looking at things'.

In this background, music and theatre then became 'crucial avenues through which criticisms of the ruling regime coalesced. As Haugerud (1995:28) argues, 'the music heavily used social and religious symbols, as well as drawing from the popular anti-colonial songs from the 1920s and the Christian hymns of the 1950s whose lyrics were altered to praise Kenyan political leaders who opposed colonial rule.'

This music carried themes that continually expressed the dissatisfaction of Kenyans towards the ruling regime. Musicians protested against the official corruption, rapid increases in the cost of living, and the government efforts to silence political opposition. There were scathing political lyrics that were evident in the music. These expressive forms, like music and theatre, Haugerud (1995:28) argues, 'create, as well as enact political understanding and consciousness'. The government was uncomfortable with these expressive forms and made attempts to ban the music. However, the artists and their audiences alike found creative channels for expressing versions of current history that differed from official scripts.

One of the channels they appropriated was to play the music in public transport vans, known as *matatus;* they would play music in bars and in shops. The informal sector vendors and street hawkers were also instrumental in the sale and distribution of this music. But while not overtly political, the themes carried in most of these songs were themselves a pointer to the disillusionment of the Kenyans.

The musicians in voicing their concerns of a united Kenya and highlighting the tribulations of the ordinary person had sensed that there was 'no room for exchange of political views: any communication [was] in essence a dialogue of the deaf' (Kariuki, 1996:70). Rather than engage with the politician, the artist opted for just naming and shaming the injustices[7]. Cultural performances are important tools especially for the marginalized. In Conquergood (1991:189) words:

> Through cultural performances, many people both construct and participate in "public" life. Particularly for the poor and marginalized people denied access to middle class "public" forums, cultural performance becomes the venue for public discussion of vital issues central to their communities as well as an arena for gaining visibility.

Though not explicitly denouncing the disillusionment, unlike most artists, musicians found subtle ways of raising the concerns of the hurly-burly of everyday politics in Kenya. Messages of corruption, tribal cleansing, and dysfunctional democracy amongst other concerns filtered through most lyrics of the songs. In agreement with Christopher Waterman (1990:8) and John Chernoff (1979:154),[8] the argument made here is that African popular musics have been broadly conditioned by competition within colonial and postcolonial economies. As Barber (1987:4) puts it, it is 'under conditions of pervasive political and economic change that music continues to play a crucial role as a medium of symbolic transaction and a means of forging and defending communities'.

A clear illustration is Joseph Kariuki's song, *Nongainūkia Itaha* (I Will Definitely Take Home my Share). While dealing with the disillusionment in urban life, the musician touches on many other issues affecting the ordinary Kenyan, while expressing some sense of resignation:

> *Ngai nowe woma* - It is only God, who will help me,
> *Ingĩkeruta* Nairobi - if I survive in Nairobi,
> *Tondū nĩ ndia ndiku* - the deep part of the river
> *Yanorĩra andū aingĩ* - that has drowned many.

Kariuki also offers some cautionary advice:

> *Korwo no mūkĩnjigue* -If you can listen to me
> *Wĩra mūndū araruta* - wherever you are working,
> *Ūtangĩruta na kĩyo* - if you don't work extra hard
> *Tondū gūtirĩ kwega* – because no job is better than any other
> *Ona ūrĩ ndingirii ūtarĩ na mbeca no tūhū* - you are just useless with a university degree and no money.

Thus, with urban disillusionment, salient issues like unemployment (the mention of a university degree) are highlighted and poses a pointer that education, especially in the 1990s has become more of a futility in the hope of ameliorating one's livelihood. It is also through the understanding that in Moi's cronyism, merit had no place[9].

Bakari (2002:4) captures best the rule of the thumb for appointments in public office during Moi's regime:

> Putative loyalty was the sole criterion for selection and appointment to lucrative public office ... some barely literate cronies were appointed to ministerial positions at the expense of the more competent, better educated and qualified individuals who did not meet his own criteria.

By highlighting the concerns that affect the ordinary Kenyan, Kariuki's song provides a window to the operations of the government of the day. Though not explicitly, the musician faults the educational policy, when a university degree cannot put food on the table. Again, it also points to the failures of the government, where state officials, appointed through the cronyism system, not through merit, "were just yes-men to the president; the type that 'Lenin described as *useful idiots*" ", (Bakari, 2002:3).

While invoking the divine intervention, Kariuki also suggests to the audience that they too have a role to shape their very own destiny in life. The refrain emphasizes the sanctuary of home, in this case the rural village the musician hails from.

Mami, njeterera, na ūhoere Ngai nongainūkia itaha
Mother, wait for me, pray for me, for I will definitely take home my share.

Home or the village is where the artist will take the loot, money he has gained from the town. The town, though seen as place for earning a living, has all its entrapments. 'Going home' for the character is escaping from the entrapments of the city and ensuring that all that is earned is not in vain, the mother in the village will be a beneficiary.

Serious concerns like the economic mismanagement, (for father has spread poverty countrywide) referring to the leadership, and the AIDS scourge (I heard them say that the maize has been poisoned)[10] alludes to Street's assertion that much as the music is some form of resistance, it can also work within the system, putting pressure on it by exciting popular feelings of concern or compassion. This chapter thus is an, attempt to understand these meanings behind the thick descriptions, behind the ordinary narratives presented in the popular music. The mention of the AIDS pandemic in the song is also an expression of concern towards the health sector which was run down a in the 1990s and the AIDS phenomenon that grew rapidly for lack of proper and sufficient health facilities.

Kimani Gecau (1991:84-5) acknowledges the contribution of popular music in commenting on and analysing the post-independence Kenyan situation and in the collective worldview and consciousness; 'popular songs have been a chronicle of the changing social situations and the relations thereof'. He adds that most of the songs have commented on the popular subject of the commoditization of all that was previously sacred, e.g., love and sex.

In line with Gecau's argument, another prevalent theme in most of the songs is that of good-time girls, which epitomises the commoditization of love. Joseph Kariuki advises men who decide to go and work in Nairobi city:

Tūirītu twī Nairobi tūhana munīko - there is a flood of young girls in Nairobi
Ūngiuga nī mwendana -If you think you are in love,
Nīūhenetie ngoro - that is self-deception
No tikwenda nī mbia - I don't blame them, it's the love for money
Ciamathūkirie mītwe - Which has dominated their thinking

Which Peter Kigia warns in a different song:

Wona mūndū - If you see a girl
Agīkwīringīrīria o mūthenya - forcing herself on to you daily
Mwehererere- Please avoid her at all costs
Akuanītie magambo - She is laden with ills
Ona arīa mena gathia – Even those with the 'worm'[11]
Matirī label - Do not have tags.

On the surface, the selected stanzas of the two different songs sound like advisory lyrics, endeavouring to advise men on how to handle the so called good-time girls in the cities. In this sense, the music seems to serve a very didactic and functional purpose to the audience; don't do this and that! But on a different veneer, nagging questions which demand answers arise; why is there a rush of young girls to the city? Why are they after material wealth and not love? Why should a woman force herself to fall in love with a man?

The two songs above, and their thematic concerns, inadvertently point out to the consequences of the deteriorating economic conditions in the 1990s which threatened the cores and standards of morality in the society. With the falling prices in export commodities like coffee, there was an influx of young people into the major towns in search of a better livelihood.

In the two songs, therefore, we tend to see the phenomenon of the good-time girls, as a response to the pervasive economic crises. Musicians, like authors, engage in the construction of symbolic economies and transforming real economic relationships into symbolic ones and helping to generate explanations of (mis)fortune that will touch the experiences of their listeners. Through such lyrics, listeners can rationalise their own poverty. After all, as Kariuki contends in his song:

Baba nĩahurunjĩte thĩna bũrũri wothe - For father has spread poverty countrywide

The 'father' in the song alludes, not only to the head of state, but also to his government for the rise of poverty in the country, for the mismanagement of resources and high unemployment cases, which led many to the streets as hawkers, as sung by another musician, Queen Jane. The 2002 Human Rights Watch Report noted that about half of Kenya's workers made their living in the informal economy as street hawkers, roadside vendors at stalls (kiosks), and as bus touts, maids, garbage scavengers, prostitutes or casual labourers. 'The government has few official policies dealing with the informal sector and workers on the, margins of society are vulnerable to arbitrary and harsh treatment by the authorities' (2002:20). Queen Jane's lament of the plight of the hawkers is symbolic of the many struggles that a great proportion of Kenyans were going through. Such lyrics offer critique to officialdom for the everyday problems of the non-elite and elite listeners alike.

When arap Moi took over from Kenyatta, he vowed to follow in his (*Nyayo*) footsteps. Kenyatta as the first president was 'the universally accepted "father of the nation"' (Kariuki, 1996:75) and Moi in line with following the footsteps inherited the title as well, as '*Baba wa taifa*' (Father of the nation). This is what the musician alludes to in the song. Bayart's (1993:87) position on postcolonial leadership in African states is that 'the link between holding positions of power within the State apparatus and the acquisition of wealth is clearly related to the political hierarchy.' Thus, in its attempts to acquire and accumulate wealth, the general populace is left wallowing in poverty, in this predator-prey relationship. What more apt way to capture this than in the musician's own words, 'father has spread poverty countrywide'? The father figure is supposed to be the benevolent provider and custodian of the domestic space. It is ironic here that instead of being the provider, the "father" is the source of poverty.

Social stratification is also expressed in characteristic metaphors and imageries drawn from the lives and experiences of the people. Highlighting the plight of hawkers on Nairobi streets, Queen Jane offers a glimpse of the tribulations by hawkers, where, striving to free themselves from the shackles of unemployment, were frustrated by the political dispensation of the day. State apparatus is exemplified by the Nairobi City Council *askaris* who endlessly harass the hawkers. Some of these street vendors were selling cassettes that contained songs that were critical of the government of the day. The hawkers thus became targets of state officials, who were bent to get rid of the banned cassettes as seen earlier. As authorities demolished informal sector kiosks and removed hawkers from Nairobi streets, their actions often provoked battles between government security forces and vendors.

It was, however, ironical that despite an emphasis by the government of the day to its polity to venture into self-employment, such efforts were thwarted by the very system. The musician illustrates the social stratum graphically and metaphorically when she queries the humanity of the *askaris*:

Andũ aya ngũria maciarirwo nĩ atumia - Are these people born of women?
Kana nĩ nyamũ cia gĩthaka - or of wild animals?
Kana nĩ rũciaro rũrĩa rwa Cain - Or are they descendants of Cain

Rworagire Habiri - Who killed Abel
Rūkīrumwo nī Ngai - And they were cursed by God

The dehumanising act by the policemen on the hawkers in this song goes beyond the social stratification. To the singer, it is not even an issue of class. She doesn't expect human beings to treat fellow humans in that regard. The spineless and ruthless character of the powers that be is laid bare. This may lead one to think about the state as a "repressor of desires"[12]. The hopelessness of the situation comes clear when the musician decides to intercede on behalf of the hawkers to God.

The suffering of the man on the street is linked to the plight of the Israelites in Egypt as narrated in the Holy Scriptures:

Ngai teithia - God help
Hawkers ciothe cia Nairobi -all the Nairobi hawkers
Mateithie ciana ciao - Help them so that their children
Itikanararīre -will never starve
Ūmarute Misri - Rescue them from Egypt
Ūmatware Canaan - Take them to Canaan

Canaan, the land of milk and honey, is a call of a return to economic normalcy that was experienced in the decades immediately after independence under the Kenyatta regime and the tranquillity where all could transact their business without government interference. This is a reflection of social disparity. Reacting to the same disparity, Joseph Kariuki complains of granaries that are never full:

Mami nī cia thūgūrī - We always work hard,
No itihūraga ikūūmbī -but our granaries are never full.
Ke tūtū tūnini -just take the little I have to offer you.
Ūtuīre mata gīthūri - And bless me.

All the lyrics quoted above are subtle illustrations of the artists' attempt to construct symbolic illustrations which are reflective of the tribulations of the ordinary man in everyday life but with an intention of trying to offer explanations to everyday suffering.

As Jewsiewicki (1997:440) rightly suggests:

> Song as a genre takes a more systematic interest in social questions
> and great existential problems than in political struggles. Its political
> impact is most acute when a metaphor focusing on social justice or
> social harmony meets with a political situation.

Most lyrics in the songs may be read as true, not in the sense of being
mimetic representations of reality, but rather in the sense of being
applicable to reality. Listeners, therefore, grasp essential features of
characters and situations and use them to interpret their own social
experience. As in popular fiction, in line with Barber's (1997:357)[13]
argument, 'both authors and readers acknowledge the active role of the
reader; the story is provided to help the readers make up their minds
about things'. Just like in proverbs, and characters and plots in popular
fiction, meaning of these songs is never complete until they are applied
to a concrete situation.[14]

The rural-urban divide manifests itself vividly in the selected songs.
The urban is on one hand seen as an opportune space for one to earn a
livelihood. The city offers a glimmer of hope towards economic
emancipation. Queen Jane emphasises the point in her song *Hawkers*.

Joseph Kariuki too assures her mother that even after spending many
years in Nairobi, he will definitely take home the fruits of his labour,
however meagre. This is emphasised in the refrain of the song as well as
in the title:

Mami njeterera - Mother wait for me
Na ūhoere Ngai - and pray for me
Nongainūkia itaha -For I will definitely take home my share

But the glamour of the city as well as the economic empowerment comes
with its own entrapments; the 'sea that has drowned many', as seen in
Kariuki's song earlier on. Kariuki expresses the disillusionment with
urban life. Yes, it might offer all the economic opportunities and
employment, but it still possesses the fatalistic characteristics. Kariuki
singles out prostitution and HIV/AIDS as drawbacks in the city. But the
differences between the urban and the rural moralities is symbolised
through female characters[15]. The young girls in the city, who are after

money, and not love, are contrasted with the mother in the village who is waiting for the son to return home with the bounty.

The very mention of returning home[16], back to the mother shows that the character has not drowned in the 'sea' that is the city. He has not succumbed to the moral deprivations of Nairobi, and is willing to return to the mother's hut in the village, because:

Na nyũmba ya maitũ - In my mother's house
Ndĩmũtharĩrie igunyũ – is kept clean for me

The musician here is idealising the village location. The village is portrayed as a symbolic space to 'resolve socio-economic problems' and contradictions of the urban space. The musician is at ease with the village, unlike the hawkers in Queen Jane's song, who:

Aumire mũciĩ - Have left home to make a living
Atiga ciana itarĩ gĩa kũrĩa - For their starving children
Na mwene nyũmba nĩarenda kũrĩhwo - And the landlord is expecting his rent

At the end of the month, the hawker is expected to meet certain expenses, like house rent, city council charges yet the survival in the hawking business is demeaning:

Hawkers cia Nairobi irĩaga cia ruo - Nairobi hawkers have no peace
Nĩ ihenya matwaragwo rĩa kamũtĩ -From endless chases
Nĩ thigari cia kanjũ - by the city council *askaris*
Na wona makũnyita - And once they get you,
Ũtunywo indo ciothe - they dispossess you of all your wares
Matwarĩre aka ao - And take them to their wives
Matirĩ rũkobe - Shame on them!!!

Thus the contradictions of the urban space and the sanctuary of the village are powerful themes evident in the songs discussed above.

Male-female relationships are also explored in everyday conflicts and difficulties, but also as a direct result of the politics of the 1990s in Kenya. Peter Kigia's song, *Arũme Twĩmenyerere* (Beware Fellow Men) captures the complaints, unfulfilled desires, broken promises, separation and loss in a love relationship between a man and a woman. The musician, representing the male gender tips fellow men on the intricacies of love relationships with modern girls:

Arũme rũrũ nĩ rwanyu - Men, this song is for you
Ndĩmũcanũre - Let me enlighten you
Matukũ tũrĩ -These days
Mũndũ ekwendwo ehũge - we have to be very careful
To kĩrĩa watũngana - Don't 'consume' whatever
Nakĩo ũgaikia kanua –we come across

Kigia is castigating the hypocrisy and the unfaithfulness in relationships. He compares the women to the Biblical Delilah who conquered the robust Samson. On the other hand though, the song is a condemnation of the craze for material wealth in the wider polity. The musician rejects the girl's overtures to love him forcibly for he is aware that there is a catch:

Arũme twĩmenyerere -Men let's beware
Aa Delilah - of modern day Delilahs
Tondũ ihinda nĩikinyu -Because the time is now,
Delilah arũnde Samson - for Delilah to knock Samson down

Kigia's advice to his fellow men:

Rĩmwe nĩmerĩrithagia - Some will come with crocodile tears
Na tũmawara - and a bag of tricks
Menya nĩguo mũtego - Know that that is their trap,
Wao Madelila- these modern Delilahs
Ona arĩra iria – Even when she cries milk, instead of tears,
Reke agakuĩre mbere - just forget about her

Such lyrics are crudely anti-women and gender insensitive. It should be noted that there is a historical basis, outside the scope of this research, to the gender politics of the Gĩkũyũ community. But it is also true that that most of these musicians rely a lot on the past for lyrical inspiration. The Gĩkũyũ community traditionally relegated the women 'to the place of a being lesser than men' (Muhoro, 1997:107). In the 1920s, as earlier noted, *Mũthĩrĩgũ* was a dance to protest against colonial attitude towards female circumcision: 'women who failed to be circumcised were given pejorative names which signified their worthlessness' (Muhoro, 1997:108). Advocacy of female genital mutilation in modern days is a clear sign of violation of women's rights. Far from being a harsh tradition, it also lowers the status of women.

However, the same traditional music treated women differently on separate circumstances. Men would sing praises of their mothers but at the same time brag as to how 'they could not take advice from women who weren't wise enough to teach them some aspects of social life' (Kabira and Mutahi, 1988:21).

Tensions in gender relations emanate from the myth of origin of the Gĩkũyũ people. Initially, the community was under a matriarchal system, but 'due to harsh and capricious rule of women ... men revolted and replaced it with a patriarchal system. There was however a compromise after strong opposition from women and the clan titles hitherto retain the female names' (Wanjohi, 1997:28).

The continuous dialogue and interplay in gender and power relations is well manifested in the day-to-day lives and musicians capture this reality aptly. Jane Nyambura, popularly known as Queen Jane in musical circles is well known for her stinging lyrics against men. Her song, *Arũme Majini* (Men are Ghosts), she says, was inspired by the increasing number of rape and defilement cases in Kenya 'Everybody knows that men are turning on young girls and abusing them, that is why I composed this song to criticize them', she argues (Muganda, 2004).

As Queen Jane castigates the behaviour of men in relationships, especially that of sugar daddies, as in her song *Nĩndarega Kũhikĩra Guka* (I refuse to be married to a grandfather), male Kikuyu musicians seem to be offering responses. Sam Muraya's famous *Mama Kiwinya* scathingly attacks older women (better known as sugar mummies) who find comfort in young boys as their lovers. Laments a young man in the song:

> *Wathũkirie mũtwe na kũheaga mbeca* – you spoilt me with money
> *Ndakwĩra ngone aciari akwa ndũngĩtĩkĩra* - you never let me visit my parents
> *Kaĩ wahikirie na ndũgĩtware rũracio* – if you married me, pay the dowry
> *Mama Kiwinya, reke njeracere* – Mother of Kiwinya, let me move on
> *Mĩaka yaku nĩ yarega tũikaranie*- the relationship can't work because of our age difference.

The same is evident in Joseph Kariuki's *Nyina wa Turera*, where he says that it's wrong for a woman of 40 years to go out with a young boy of 20. The consistent dialogue between musicians across the gender divide encapsulates the day-to-day realities in the society. For Queen Jane, she is unapologetic about her hard-line stance against men; 'the fact that men are among my greatest fans simply means that I am telling the truth' (Muganda, 2004). The above underlies the fact that musicians do not deal with issues that are out of this world, but actually the daily happenings.

The HIV/AIDS scourge is another thematic concern addressed in most songs. The government has used song, music and dance to create awareness and sensitise the public about the disease. In 1999, Lilian Auma, best known as Princess Jully, emerged tops in a Kenya Music Extravaganza (Ogola, 1999: iv), with her song *Dunia Mbaya* (The Cruel World). The song rose almost to an anthem level for its advisory lyrics on AIDS and caution against promiscuity. This is an indication that AIDS is a serious theme amongst musicians. Here is a scourge, affecting people, decimating populations, and people should end promiscuity. Auma goes on to give stark details of the symptoms of the disease.

Joseph Kariuki comments on the same but by engaging in his community's idiom, maintaining what Ndebele earlier calls a semblance of social order. Kariuki makes no mention of AIDS, but by 'localising' his lyrics, sends the message home:

> *Ndīraiguire makiuga* - I heard them say
> *Atī mbembe nī ndoge* - that the 'maize' has been poisoned
> *Mūndū ohe ngui yake* - Keep your 'dog' in the kernel,
> *Wega ndīkarie thumu* - lest it consumes poison
> *Mami ndūgakīnduīre* - So mother, do not blame me
> *Wona itarī na mūka* - if I am not married
> *Kwī mūrimū ūkīte* - There is a new disease,
> *Na kwīgita ti guoya* - and self-defence is not cowardice[17]

Kariuki's use of the dog and maize metaphors is crucial. The dog metaphor is ascribed to men, while women take the maize metaphor. Whilst men are seen as dogs, women are portrayed as the 'poisoned maize'. Cleverly, the musician steers away from any conclusive remark as to whether men or women are to shoulder the blame for the scourge. To the musician, a vicious dog is as dangerous as poison; men and women alike are equally to blame for the spread of AIDS and HIV. But as discussed below, the Gĩkũyũ community is highly patriarchal, like most African societies. The allusion to women as 'maize' to be 'consumed' and men as 'dogs', the 'consumer' depicts clearly the gender and power relations, which is characterized by some predator/prey axis. The dog can denote any kind of predator, whilst maize is any prey.

However, Kariuki, by drawing this analogy addresses a serious theme through an appropriation of the community's repertoire. This relationship between consumption and sexual pleasure is interesting. But all Kariuki stresses here is that people should take care; AIDS is on the rampage and people should be concerned. While claiming that 'he heard them say that maize has been poisoned', he is trying to pose and ponder questions over the myths and origins of the disease.

From the discussion on thematic concerns in the songs, it comes out clearly that the poet/singer and the addressee are typical, 'yet ordinary people with whom the man on the street (or the man in the bar) can identify; vicariously, the song expresses their experiences and feelings' (Fabian, 1978:326).

Some songs try to offer solutions to listeners. This is done by going beyond the 'spectacle' in order to reveal the necessary knowledge of actual reality so that we can purposefully deal with it. As Ndebele (1991:50) asserts, a narrative should be a demonstration of its own intentions. Songs should not just be seen to bring out graphic illustrations of suffering, but also try and suggest possibilities of coming out of the predicament. This is when a song may be said to be tackling the real issues of everyday living; speaking of the ordinary. Ndebele argues that it is this portrayal of the ordinary that contradicts the spectacle and brings out the reality on the ground: 'The ordinary is sobering rationality; it is the forcing of attention on necessary detail' (1991:50).

Although there is a penchant towards the apolitical, e.g. in domestic scenes, social functions, the underlying themes are clear messages of concern to the audience or the community. Though not outright overt in their lyrics, clear contours of political disaffection can be gleaned.

Worth noting from the above quote is that distinct differences are noticeably gleaned between traditional music and popular music. It is true that unlike the traditional musician, contemporary musician much as being a commentator of the politics of daily life also thinks of music as his sole means of livelihood.

How the music is received and interpreted is quite vital while reconsidering the themes treated in the various songs that have been analysed. What this means here is that while theorizing the audience, we are looking at how people receive, interpret and use music both as a cultural form and a means of entertainment while engaging in specific social activities. What this chapter is really keen on is that the same musical genre or piece of music may be enjoyed and engaged with in completely different ways. Quite different audience experiences and activities as Negus, (1997:32), argues 'are associated with listening to the same music in a performance event in stadia, while driving or jogging with a Walkman, or while dancing to a juke box in an open-air- bar'.

In a fieldwork research, in the interior parts of Central Kenya, inhabited by the Gĩkũyũ community, it was clear that the most popular songs amongst patrons were not even from Gĩkũyũ artistes. Excusing the limitations of the song selections (most of them are Kikuyu songs anyway!) in the jukebox, the most popular song was '*Paulo My Lover*', by Kalenjin Sisters. Apart from the refrain which is in English, the rest was in the Nandi dialect which none of the patrons could hardly understand. But it was one song, which got patrons squeeze in the dance floor at the top of their voices dancing. To emphasise Negus' point above that the kind of social activity the audience is involved in, determines how they receive any kind of music.

Much as music is closely related to cultural identity, the meaning of music changes (both at home and away) as it moves out from its point of origin, to other parts of the world. This illustrates, 'ways in which music can be used as a means of transcending the limitations of our own place in the world, of constructing trajectories rather than boundaries across space' (Stokes, 1994:4).

Identification with a song out of the audience's immediate comprehension, from a different community is seen here as providing the means by which the ethnic community can transform themselves to assume a more national outlook. In Stokes' (1994:4) words, for a rural folk identifying with urban genres gives them avenues through which 'rural-urban migrants can transform themselves from peripheralised proletarians to urbanites, "become" members of the "clean" middle class, become members of groups which represent in some way or another, specific migrants interests'.

This relationship between music and society, however, is not a one-way exchange, given the complexities of the postcolony. With the 'chaotic plurality' (Mbembe, 2001:104) that characterises the postcolony, it would be necessary to explore the partisan and ambiguous nature of music and musicians in Kenya. This stems from the understanding that music is not always a site of subversion, but can also be manipulated by both the citizenry and the officialdom to suit their interests, as is the case in the following chapter.

Notes

[1] This study acknowledges that there is a corpus of music from the Gīkūyū community; from the traditional genres to the modern beat in the 21st century. It is also true that in the decade under review, many other artists from the community continually produced songs. The few chosen are just a representation of the themes that the scope of this research could allow.

[2] Bodil FolkeFrederiksen, 'Joe, the Sweetest Reading in Africa: Documentation and Discussion of a Popular Magazine in Kenya' in Stephanie Newell's *Readings in African Popular Fiction*. Oxford: James Currey, 2002, p 94. It's worth noting that Frederiksen's paper, though largely discussing a public magazine in Kenya becomes quite relevant in a discussion of popular arts, including music.

[3] With the repeal of the repressive Section 2A in 1991, Kenyans welcomed the re-introduction of multiparty democracy. The country had become a *de jure* one-party state in 1982, a move by President Moi to entrench his dictatorial tendencies and crackdown on real or perceived political enemies.

[4] KANU (Kenya African National Union) was the ruling party under Mzee Jomo Kenyatta, and one that reigned immediately after independence until December 2002 when the party lost to a coalition of opposition parties, NARC (National Rainbow Coalition). In subsequent mentions, the party will only be referred by its acronym, KANU.

[5] Mwakenya is an acronym for *Muungano wa Wazalendo wa Kuikomboa Kenya*, literally translated as 'The Progressive Movement to Liberate Kenya'. According to Maina wa Kinyatti in his memoirs, *Kenya: A Prison Notebook*, (London, Vita Books, 1996:169), it was an underground revolutionary movement started in the 1970s. Originally it was

referred to as the 'December Twelfth Movement', before it changed to Mwakenya. A crackdown on the movement by the Government led to the arrest of mainly university lecturers, students and their leaders and later of other professionals.

[6] See Korwa Adar and Isaac Munyae, (2001:8) who aver that the government instigated the ethnic violence in order to portray the multi-party systems as inappropriate for Kenya.

[7] Barber, (1997:5) argues that in naming a common suffering, there is always an aspiration to a better life.

[8] Chernoff and Waterman argue that music is essential to life in Africa because Africans use music to mediate their involvement within a community. They further agree that the very act of naming a genre may be a declaration of cultural consolidation.

[9] The Kenyan president Daniel Arap Moi, known for his skimpy academic standards declared himself "Professor of Politics" and said he 'could teach people like Professor Anyang' Nyong'o, [an actual political scientist and presently a Minister in the regime of Mwai Kibaki] something about politics' as Outa notes in his article "*Lysistrata* in Nairobi: Performing Power of Womanhood in the Postcolony" in *African Studies, 58:2*, 1999, p 207.

[10] Lyrics alluding to HIV/AIDS and poverty appear later in the chapter.

[11] Worm is metaphorically used here to mean HIV/AIDS

[12] Simon Gikandi, in Anna Rutherford's (ed) *From Commonwealth to Postcolonial*. Sydney: Dangaroo Press, 1992, argues that in the postcolonial situation, the nation is not the manifestation of a common interest but a repressor of desires, p 380.

[13] Karin Barber, "Preliminary Notes on Audiences in Africa", *Africa*, 67, 3, 1997

[14] Stephanie Newell (2002:5) argues that different categories of people extract different models from texts and performances. Audiences take sides with the character type whose social position most closely resembles their own. See "Paracolonial Networks, The Rise of Literary and Debating Societies in Colonial West Africa", *Literary Culture in Colonial Ghana, 'How to Play the Game of Life'*, Bloomington, Indiana University Press, 2002, p. 5.

[15] Stephanie Newell (2002:7) argues that perhaps it is easier to criticize women's behaviour more readily and safely than that of the national political class, and that female morality is more manageable than political corruption in Africa.

[16] However, the space called home comes with its own complexities. Marangoly (1996:9) defines home as the 'desired place that is fought for and established as the exclusive

domain of a few' (p 9). She however acknowledges that home is both a place to escape to and a place to escape from'. There are contradictions and ambiguities of this space normally referred to as home. For more on politics and poetics of home, see Marangoly (1996), and Mutonya (2001).

[17] An English equivalent to this proverb would be 'prevention is better than cure'.

CHAPTER THREE

Praise and Protest: Music and Contesting Patriotisms in Postcolonial Kenya

This chapter explores the partisan nature of music and musicians in Kenya from the colonial era to the present and investigates how music served many different sectarian interests during this period. It reveals how the ambivalent space within which musicians work influences and shapes their music, paying particular attention to the political context. It shows how officialdom in postcolonial Kenya has endeavoured to construct and then saturate public space with its own version of patriotism. However, the fact that, in the economic and political context of contemporary Kenya, some musicians defend their right to economic gain in response to accusations of sycophancy, suggests that popular music does not always function as a site of subversion.

> 'We pray for our president, Daniel arap Moi.
> Moi cannot stop corruption, so help him God.
> Moi cannot even stop the formation of opposition parties.
> So God help the president before he is thrown into the lion's den'.

The above song by Joseph Kamaru is not the only instance of serious political issues being contested through music in Kenya. For more than half a century, music has functioned as a fundamental mode of the expression and enactment of politics. From the colonial period through to 1963, when Kenya became independent with Jomo Kenyatta as its first president, to the second republic, during Daniel arap Moi's reign (1978-2002), to the present moment under Mwai Kibaki, the musician has played a significant role in providing a commentary on contemporary politics.

The past three decades in particular have witnessed major political upheaval in Kenya: from the 1982 attempted coup to political assassinations of Tom Mboya, J.M Kariuki, Robert Ouko among others and ethnic clashes of 1991-1998; from the stigmatisation of intellectuals and perceived dissidents to the introduction of political pluralism as opposed to the one-party state system. Throughout this period, music has consistently functioned as one of the most salient sites of struggle between rulers and ordinary people. One of the reasons for this is that music is one of most important modes through which ordinary Kenyans express their wishes, identities and aspirations. It is arguably the most important aspect of the country's popular culture.

Particularly with regard to the interface between popular culture and politics, this study regards the popular as a political moral category, 'the definition of the popular being that which functions in the interests of the masses (the farmers, workers, unemployed) by opening up their eyes to their own objective, historical situation, the actual conditions of their existence and thus enabling themselves to empower themselves' (Barber, 1997:5) As Johannes Fabian (1978:315) similarly asserts, popular culture:

> signifies potentially at least processes occurring behind the back of established powers and accepted interpretations and thus offers a better conceptual approach to decolonisation of which it is undoubtedly an important element.

However, this research does not view these cultural expressions simply as mirrors of a society or a nation. . Although this function should not be ignored, cultural productions should not only be seen as reflections or reflexes of political, social and economic conditions. As Keith Negus (1997:4) posits, music as a form of cultural expression cannot simply reflect a society, an individual's personality, a city or the age we live in:

> The word reflection is one that slips very easily into both academic discourse and everyday conversations about popular music. But no music can be a mirror to capture events or activities in its melodies, rhythms and voices. The world, a society, an individual life or even a particular incident is far too complex for any cultural product (book, film or song) to be able to capture and spontaneously reflect. Music is created, circulated, recognized and responded to according to a range of conceptual assumptions and analytical activities that are grounded in quite particular social relationships, political processes and cultural activities.

This chapter then considers ways in which two types of music that have been considered popular in Kenya have both reflected and enacted various forms of national politics. The first type is of popular music is the commercial music played by professional musicians, usually in a group with a guitar band-style line up, and recorded to be disseminated through the mass media and sold on records, cassettes or compact discs. The second type of popular music considered here is choral music, sung by relatively large groups of people, often amateurs. Choral music is sometimes recorded for broadcast and sale, although not always.

Though the choral music is not necessarily Gīkūyū music, this music is read as counter-narratives from the state, and as they are presented as strategies of state-sponsored patriotism. These songs rose to almost the status of national culture. It is important to touch on them as they provide a template for the genre of praise songs in Kenya. However, this analysis takes cognisance of the fact that the praise genre has been in existence in pre-colonial Gīkūyū community.

Merger between the two types mentioned above occurs when a commercially recorded band song is taken up by an interest group and becomes a popular anthem sung in a communal, almost choral style when that group comes together. The study investigates how this popular music has existed alongside historical and political changes. Whereas the popular music has offered alternative means of challenging the status quo, examples are draw from the instances where music has been used as political propaganda. The main argument in this chapter is that music is a site for power contestation in postcolonial Kenya.

In the years between the 1930s and the late 1950s, during the Kenyan struggle for independence from colonial rule, and also during the Mau Mau war in the 1950s, a genre of music evolved that functioned to articulate a vision of a postcolonial Kenya and to affirm a sense of pride, identity and community amongst black Kenyan peasants and workers. Song and dance functioned in an emancipatory manner because it enabled people to share their burdens, triumphs and gladness of heart by singing about the common oppressor and exploiter; the colonialist. It drew people together and united them in one common aim, goal or purpose. As the South African Black Consciousness Movement leader Steve Biko (1979:60) asserted, song and dance is able to 'promote a culture of defiance, group pride, self-assertion and solidarity that emanates from a situation of common experience of oppression and is responsible for the restoration of our faith in ourselves'.

During the Kenyan struggle for independence and through the following decades, music served to unite and mobilize the masses of ordinary Kenyans at times when the welfare and stability of the community was in jeopardy. Though varied in modes of expression, the peoples' reaction to communal crisis is strikingly similar throughout the years under colonialism and after. During the Mau Mau, for instance, song was used consistently to nag, cajole, and implore the Gĩkũyũ community to fight for their dignity and identity. Ngugi wa Thiong'o shows that during the colonial period, *Mũthĩrĩgũ* and *Kanyegenyũri* dances were utilised by anti-colonial forces to express resistance. He goes on to demonstrate that culture in Kenya has long been an important theatre of political confrontation, enumerating a number of colonial and postcolonial cultural productions that arose in response to political repression (1993:88).

Maina wa Kinyatti's work on songs sang during the Mau Mau period demonstrates the saliency of Barber's argument regarding the use of popular culture as a mobilising tool. Wa Kinyatti shows that within a span of five years, Mau Mau produced a most formidable body of political songs[1], which was used by the movement as a weapon to politicise and educate Kenyan workers and peasants. He argues that 'this helped heighten the people's consciousness against the forces of the foreign occupiers and in the process prepared them for armed struggle' (1980:xii). He argues that the role played by these songs in educating workers and peasants and mobilising them against dictatorship of the colonialists was a vital catalyst in the development and success of the movement.

Although wa Kinyatti's perspective is anchored in a Marxist interpretative paradigm, his approach to the study of music as a form of cultural and political expression is relevant to this inquiry. His argument is, however, flawed in a number of ways. First, like many Kenyan musicians discussed below, wa Kinyatti formulates a 'powerful vision of confraternity in suffering' (Barber 1997:5). This entails a generic assumption that peasants and workers are one homogenous group. Secondly, the assumption that this category of people is in need of education and politicisation far more than other social classes is arguable. Such a claim does not acknowledge the peasants' agency. The argument here is that these songs during the Mau Mau resonated with and articulated the peasants' grievances, the latter were not educated and politicised through song from above. After all, it was the nature of their political awareness that created the impulse to compose these songs in the first instance.

Writing on nationalism and peasant consciousness in India, Partha Chatterje argues that the peasant consciousness has its own paradigmatic from which is in fact the antithesis of the bourgeoisie consciousness. The peasant consciousness, he argues, 'cannot be understood in its own constitutive aspects if it is reduced to the bourgeoisie rationality' (1993:163-4). To deny them the agency as wa Kinyatti posits above would condemn the peasants to the conception that they are 'poor, ignorant, unthinking and subject to unreasonable excitements', cautions Chatterjee (1986:149). The sound argument here is that the peasants too had their own knowledge of their sufferings and interests, and that the songs only reiterated and re-emphasised their plight, and not necessarily heightened their consciousness against the colonial forces. Wa Kinyatti also portrays stark binaries between colonizers and colonized when the situation was more complex.

In 1963, Kenya attained independence and Jomo Kenyatta became the country's first president. The resistance songs of the Mau Mau era became songs of celebration that were commonly performed by formal ensembles at official functions and events. Making reference to two songs[2] which highlighted Kenyatta's tribulations at the same time valorising his suffering, Ogude (2003:277) argues that Kenyatta turned his praise songs into a daily ritual that all 'patriotic Kenyans were expected to defer to without deviation. Almost every news bulletin was preceded by one or the other praise song to Kenyatta'. Kenyatta cashed in on his popularity at the moment immediately after independence, but which later waned in the years that followed. Kenyatta also had a retinue of traditional *Nyakīnyua* women dancers as well as mass choirs to entertain him wherever he was addressing rallies or even at the State House.

It is in the period immediately after independence that the first praise songs composed by pop musicians began to emerge. One of the most famous of these was CDM Kiratu's *Mūgathe Jomo Kenyatta* (His Excellency Jomo Kenyatta), which was recorded in the early 1970s. The central figure in Gīkūyū commercial popular music in the 1960s and 1970s, the period of Kenyatta's presidency, was, however, Joseph Kamaru. An analysis of his music is presented in the following chapter.

Kamaru sang both songs praising the Kenyatta regime, as well as those that were critical of the establishment.

When Daniel arap Moi took power in 1978 one of his primary strategies was to emphasise and gain the most benefit possible from the praise side of the praise poet tradition. In 1979, Moi instigated the formation of his premiere propaganda ensemble, the Muungano Choir, a mass choir whose membership represented the diversity of Kenyan society. The President's enthusiasm for, and support of, this kind of music stimulated many state corporations to form their own choirs – all of which sang the praises of the KANU party and President Moi.

Years later, in a newspaper interview after Moi's departure, Muungano Choir director Boniface Mgangha asserted that his choir was unique in that it had to represent the aspirations of the country at the time. He says that Muungano's objective was to sing patriotic songs as part of the broader role to enhance socio-politico development. He cites *Kenya, Kipenzi Changu* (Kiswahili: Kenya, My Love) by his choir as the most remarkable recording in its genre. The formation of government-sponsored choirs is a classic example of what Martin Stokes (1994:10) describes as the intensive involvement of music as a tool in the hand of new states to propagate the dominant modes of classification.

The first three years of the Moi era saw the recording of a large body of pro-Moi and KANU praise songs that came to form a new genre termed 'patriotic songs'. Performed both by choirs and by commercial popular musicians, these songs enjoyed extensive airplay on the Kenya Broadcasting Corporation radio and TV (then the only broadcasting station, which was under strict government control) over the following two decades. Some of the most famous patriotic songs recorded by commercial bands included *Rais Moi* (Kiswahili: President Moi) by the Kenya-based Congolese band Mangelepa; *Hongera Moi* (Kiswahili: Congratulations Moi") by Them Mushrooms, a popular music group, now renamed Uyoga Band; Joseph Kamaru's *Safari ya Japan* (Kiswahili: Trip to Japan)[3] and *Chunga Marima* (Watch your Steps).

Despite all President Moi's efforts to retain control over the political power of music, unmitigated praise of his government by musicians was not to last. In 1982, Kenya faced the first attempted military *coup d'etat*, which lasted only a few hours. Hundreds lost their lives, and much property was destroyed. This precipitated a deluge of songs. One of these, *Kenya ya Ngai* (Kenya Belongs to God), starts:

> *Nĩ Kenya ĩrĩa yakwa ndahũrangĩrwo?*
> *Kana nĩ ĩrĩa itũ mwahunyĩrĩra?*
> *Yainainio ta thaara ta ĩtarĩ mwene*
> *Kuma ũmũthĩ ngũmĩne Ngai*

> Is it the Kenya I suffered for?
> Or is it our Kenya you play around with?
> Which had been shaken like it belongs to no one?
> From now onwards I deliver it to God

The song castigates politicians who get into power just to enrich themselves:

> *Ngũigua ta ingĩrĩra ndaririkana*
> *Tũgũikĩirie mĩtĩ ũgatũtetere*
> *Na rĩu nĩ Kenya woha mũgoto*
> *Ngũria ũkũmĩendia kũ Kenya ya Ngai*

> I feel like crying when I remember
> We voted you into power to represent our interests
> And now you intend to sell Kenya
> Where shall you sell this Kenya of God?

The song then challenges the politicians by asking them whether they have no mercy, for the children, the women, and the aged who suffer as a result of power-hungry leaders. The song concludes by warning politicians that if they were in Nairobi during the time of 'Power' (the attempted coup) then they would know that power is God-given.

The coup heralded a period of intense political repression of those who critiqued the state. In music this manifested most obviously in heavy censorship. *Kenya ya Ngai,* for instance, was never given airplay by the only broadcasting station at the time, Kenya Broadcasting Corporation (KBC) because, Mucoki (1992:18) asserts, 'the policy makers felt that these songs and others with similar lyrics were undermining their positions'.

Writing on politics and popular culture largely in Europe and America, John Street (1997:77) argues that 'artistic creativity depends upon the freedom of expression to which state interference is antithetical'. In many postcolonial states, however, there are many instances of state censorship of popular culture. Typically, this indicates the existence of an authoritarian regime. During apartheid for instance, the South African government banned countless books, plays, songs, and films and as Street (1997:86) notes about a different context, 'the Nazis took particular exception to "swing youth", a group of young bourgeoisie, who chose to dance to the "decadent Jewish" and "degenerate" prohibited music of Benny Goodman, Louis Armstrong, amongst other giants of the age of jazz'. The interference of the state in the form of censorship constitutes negative political power: 'the power to prevent' (Street 1997:88). Power, Street argues, can also be used to facilitate what the audience listens to, where, through broadcasting policies, the audience is made to discriminate actively rather than to be entertained passively. In this way, state decisions influence popular culture and the ambiguities and complexities between popular culture and politics are highlighted. The ambiguity is more pronounced by the thought that 'the quality of cultural life is important to the quality of political life. This parallels a general argument about the relationship between democracy and the system of broadcasting' (Street, 1997:97).

Despite censorship and other authoritarian measures taken in attempt to silence his opposition, President Moi ultimately lost the battle and was forced to accept multi-party politics. Music, amongst many other factors, was central in achieving this end. Commenting on the changing and volatile political tide that swept through Kenya in the early 1990s, Haugerud (1995:28) notes that music and theatre became important avenues through which criticisms of the ruling regime 'coalesced, influencing individual consciousness' as the opposition grew bigger and became more public by late 1991 and early 1992:

> Some of the music built on earlier expressive forms, such as popular anti-colonial songs from the 1920s and Christian hymns sung in the 1950s whose words were altered to praise Kenyan political leaders who opposed colonial rule. In 1992, Kenyan mothers of political prisoners protesting publicly at Nairobi law courts sang Gĩkũyũ funeral songs.

In the 1990s, the period heralding the introduction of multi-party politics in Kenya, several Gĩkũyũ popular musicians released songs that the authorities deemed subversive. Such songs included the following, all by Albert Gacheru: *Mũcemanio wa Nyamũ* (Meeting of the animals), *Thĩna wa Muoroto* (The Troubles of Muoroto), *Mathĩna ma Matiba* (Matiba's Tribulations).[4] The song *Thĩna wa Muoroto* (which refers to Muoroto, a slum in the outskirts of Nairobi that was demolished by government authorities) contains strong metaphors relating the demolition of the shanties to the works of Satan. In the song a voice asks Satan what kind of leaders he prefers in this world and Satan answers: 'I like the cruel ones, those who have no heart for the poor and the children. Those who are not willing to alleviate suffering of their people.' The musician, Albert Gacheru, who recorded this song was arrested by the authorities but later released. Officials said that the Muoroto song was, 'calculated to cause disaffection among Kenyans, and was a threat to state security, peace and order' (Haugerud 1995:30).

Joseph Kamaru's song *Mahoya ma Bũrũri* (Prayers for the Nation) was also banned, and Kamaru was held by the police for questioning. The lyrics included the following:

> We pray for our president, Daniel arap Moi.
> Moi cannot stop corruption, so help him God.
> Moi cannot even stop the formation of opposition parties.
> So God help the president before he is thrown into the lion's den.

Haugerud (1995:28-9) confirms that the popular music cassettes that the government termed seditious circulated amongst a wide audience in Kenya in the early 1990s:

> "Subversive" cassettes offered important alternatives to official versions of recent history'... under some historical conditions, such expressive forms may be more than a "safety valve" that allows the political status quo to continue. Under other conditions, such as those in Kenya in the early 1990s, such forms become crucial symbolic weapons in active struggles for political transformation.

Haugerud goes on to argue that popular music as a form of a cultural production elucidates 'competition for moral authority in Kenya in contemporary political struggles over who is to control the state and with what political practices and ideals' (1995:29). The wide circulation of the 'subversive' cassettes was made possible by the changes in the political arena with the inculcation of a culture of political opposition, especially after the 1990 repeal of the repressive Section 2A of the Kenyan constitution, which paved the way for multi-party politics. What the introduction of multi-party politics allowed was the voicing of conflicting versions of what the nation should be and, therefore, contesting versions of patriotism.

In its purest form, patriotism involves the loyalty that a person has towards his or her country, an affinity for a shared history of sacrifice and common values. National anthems encapsulate patriotism and normally celebrate a sense of sacred place and people and values and even a way of life that endears the citizens to their native land. Such is the kind of patriotism that was expected of citizens during the struggle for independence and immediately after; one that entailed an unconditional support of one's government. The problem with such kind of patriotism is that it didn't involve an abrogation of individual responsibility on the part of the citizen and it has also enabled governments to lead their citizenry to ruin.

Music and song has risen to the fore in each period of political transition since the Second World War. During the Mau Mau for instance, Maina wa Kinyatti asserts that songs 'tried to answer the fundamental questions in the colony: what is patriotism? And therefore who are the patriots and who are the traitors? (1980: ix). In each subsequent period of political upheaval, this question has been asked again through song. The above version of patriotism would have subtly answered such questions.

A different version of patriotism emerged with time, far more beyond the flag and the national anthem. Conflict arises when leaders are perceived as not acting in the best interests of the people. In this case, patriotic supporter of the leaders may be perceived as traitors of the people and vice versa. *Thīna wa Muoroto*, discussed above, directly declares a lack of congruence between the interests of the Kenyan government and those of its people. Patriotism here demanded the courage of one's conviction and the willingness to speak the truth as one saw it for the good of the country. When the disillusionment narrative became widely recognised as was the case in Kenya during the early 1990s, musicians who performed 'patriotic songs' suddenly found themselves being critiqued as traitors of the people. The standard of their art was also more openly critiqued. A recent press article complains for instance:

> The divide between sycophancy and art disappeared, as was the case in communist regimes. In the new genre, the 'correct' political content was all that mattered. Genuinely patriotic compositions such as *Kenya Nchi Yetu* (Kenya Our Country) were apparently too aloof. The president had to be praised or 'disgruntled elements' criticized for a song to be patriotic. Praising the motherland wasn't enough. Its leader deserved a special mention.[5]

This was patriotism as sanctioned by the regime. Although some patriotic songs recorded by commercial artists were deemed as good compositions, in many cases the content of the lyrics took precedence over musical quality. A good majority were rush recordings whose sole purpose was to pitch for attention for those in power in the hope of gaining rapport and getting some reward from the head of state or others in high office. Similarly, while some commentators suggest that, on an artistic level, the formation of in-house choirs by state corporations was a positive factor for music development nationally, others assert that such choirs were open to widespread abuse by opportunists who used them to pitch for political favours, and choir members who saw them as a means to make easy money and advance personal agendas.

Another area of scathing criticism directed at these choirs is that they altered gospel songs in order to introduce lyrics in praise of the President. The music set new, explicitly political texts to a variety of pre-existing religious compositions for the purposes of praising the governing establishment. The debasing of the Christian liturgy became an issue with the St Stephen's Choir's tribute to the late Mzee Jomo Kenyatta, when it altered lyrics in popular church hymns in order to pass them for tribute songs to the late President.[6] Most of these songs were eventually dropped from Christian worship because it was felt that they had been debased because they had acquired loaded political meanings, and praised mortal human beings instead of God. The practice of adapting Christian songs continued into the Moi era, although the resulting repertoire did not enjoy widespread exposure.

As early as the 1920s, Christian hymns[7] were corrupted by the Gĩkũyũ to suit the struggle mood. Notes Ogot, (1977: 276) 'when meetings were apparently swaying in religious fervour to the strains of "Abide With Me" or "Onward Christian Soldiers" the congregation was in reality being exhorted to fight for their independence or regain their stolen land'.

Most songs sang during the Mau Mau deviated from the religious tone of the Christian hymns (from which they derived the tunes from) to praise the heroes of the day, who were mostly Gĩkũyũ). One particular Christian hymn;

> I love to read about the past
> When Jesus was living in this earth
> And how he used to call children
> To join his flock
> How I wish I were one of them

Was corrupted to:

> I love to read about the past
> When Mũgo wa Kĩbirũ was living on this earth
> I hear his prophesy that
> The whites will come and go
> I could be happy if the whites could leave
> So that our children
> Can have a place to live in. (Ogot, 1977:281)

There was even a parodied creed in the same line as hymns, which was supposed to be said by every Gĩkũyũ after the singing of the hymns:

> I believe in God, Father Almighty
> Maker of Heaven and Earth
> And I believe in Gĩkũyũ and Mũmbi
> Our parents to whom He assigned this country
> They bore nine full clans, who were tortured from time immemorial
> During the time of Waiyaki, Chege and Wang'ombe. (Ogot: 1977:283)

'Mau Mau leaders firmly believed that their cause was sanctioned by God, who was on their side. Kenyatta was seen as the chosen one to deliver them from colonialism' Ogot (1977:283). When Kenyatta took over from the colonialists, the same praise songs, and Christian hymns altered to serve secular and political purposes continued unabated. This is one of the instances in which shifts in the political landscape either threatened the existence, or subsequently reworked the significance of particular musical practices. The protest songs of the 1950s were adapted as praise songs to the postcolonial regime.

The primary response of musicians to charges of sycophancy is that they sing about issues relevant to people and express sentiments that people identify with. In certain periods, pro-government praise songs (patriotic songs) sold well because, the argument goes, many people wished to hear them. Again, patriotism here was defined in the narrow sense of unconditional support to the government of the day.

At the height of one party dictatorship in Kenya, choirs that performed praise songs[8] to the ruling party KANU and the then president Daniel Moi were endemic features in the life of ordinary Kenyans. Such songs were played out loud after every news bulletins on the only broadcaster then, Kenya Broadcasting Corporation (state owned) on a daily basis. The trend has continued even after multi-party democracy, where state corporations and academic institutions all form part of national day celebrations every year. Their songs serve as a tool for pledging loyalty and praise to ruling regimes. At the onset of colonialism was the missionary. The missionaries and the proselytisers introduced Christian hymns with simple choruses. The choruses were widely adapted by the early mission stations and were used to teach the basic tenets. The seeds of colonial penetration of East Africa 'were planted initially in the Christian missions and schools. Music was used from the beginning in the indoctrination and the teaching of Western ideology. Songs and hymns therefore were important tools in the processes of subjugation to new moral values and systems' (Barz, 2003:57). To draw similarities between role of songs as a means of the indoctrinating western ideology by mission schools as stated above, and the praise songs in postcolonial Kenya would seem to oversimplify a complex issue, but it serves the purpose of this study. The underlying fact here is that music, and in this case, choral music is a crucial propaganda tool.

In a newspaper interview in 2002, shortly before Moi's fall from power, musician Kamaru, who featured in many public functions, officiated over by President Moi, denied that musicians were being used by the government saying that, in his case and in the case of many other artists who performed such songs, the objective was purely commercial because there was a market for songs praising Moi and KANU: "I had good sales with *Chunga Marima* because it had commercial appeal and I believe others saw it from commercial perspective". Kamaru adds that he received no reward from State House for his praise songs, but does admit that President Moi was generous to musicians singing in his functions and gave generous cash handouts.[9] When the political tables turned, President Moi similarly refused to believe that the deluge of anti-KANU songs released during the run up to the 1992 general election was a response to a market desire for the expression of such political sentiments. He distanced himself from musicians asserting that they were in the payroll of opposition parties.

One of the most salient critiques of the state of the Kenyan nation issued by a Gĩkũyũ musician in the early 2000s was Eric Wainaina's album *Sawa Sawa* (Kiswahili: All is Fine). Wainaina brings me back to the other version of patriotism, often seen in opposition to the blind loyalty to the government. This version dictates that a citizen has a duty to make an independent, reasoned judgement of whether the actions of his/her government are in the best interest of the country. Though people may have different standards and might reach different conclusions from the same fact, what matters is not that there be unanimity of beliefs but that the citizens decide for themselves whether a particular governmental course of action is in the best interest of their country. Wainaina's song, in this regard can be regarded as a patriotic song. The first track, in the album, which became a hit throughout the country, laments the level of corruption in Kenya. This song, *Nchi ya Kitu Kidogo* (Kiswahili: The Country of Something Small), is commonly translated as "The Land of Corruption". This song not only appealed to the Kenyan public, it also shot the artist into the limelight making him the co-winner of the best song, East African category, in the annual South African-based Kora[10] Awards in 2002. Within a couple of months of its release *Nchi ya Kitu Kidogo* had come to epitomize the desire of Kenyans to live in a corruption-free society.[11]

Kenya under President Daniel Moi was regularly ranked as one of the most corrupt countries in the world by anti-graft agencies like the Transparency International.[12] Also, the IMF and World Bank held back millions of dollars of aid until specific, concrete steps were taken to fight corruption. Transparency International argued that graft contributed to the high levels of poverty in most developing countries, as Peter Eigen, Chairman of the organization observed during the launch of the Corruption Perceptions Index 2002:

> Political elites and their cronies continue to take kickbacks at every opportunity. Hand in glove with corrupt business people, they are trapping whole nations in poverty and hampering sustainable development. Corruption is perceived to be dangerously high in poor parts of the world, but also in many countries whose firms invest in developing nations.

Corruption permeates all levels of Kenyan public life. *Kitu Kidogo*, which literally means "Something Small", is what ordinary people pay, on a daily basis, to grease the palms of minor bureaucrats. To be admitted to hospital, to attain a driving license, or if you get stopped by the police, you have to bribe the relevant official. Wainaina's song asserts that the problem exists absolutely everywhere:

Huko Kenyatta madawa zimeisha
Masheet zauzwa marikiti mia kwa mia ah
Wafanyikazi waenda miezi bila pesa
Ni bahati ukitibiwa

In Kenyatta National Hospital, there are no drugs
Bed sheets for hospital beds are being sold for throw away prices
Hospital staff goes for months without pay
You are lucky when you get treated

Towards the end of KANU's reign, Kenyans were becoming increasingly exasperated with corruption, especially as the economy was flagging and poverty levels were reaching insurmountable heights. Ordinary citizens blamed this predicament solely on the country's leaders, who - they said - had plundered the nation's resources. However, as citizens are not exempt from corrupt practices, the blame does not rest solely on the leaders. Describing this situation as mutual zombification, between rulers and subjects Achille Mbembe asserts:

> [T]he postcolonial relationship is not primarily a relationship of resistance or of collaboration but can be best characterized as illicit cohabitation, a relationship made fraught by the very fact of the

commandment and its 'subjects' having to share the same living space. (1992:4)

Kenyan people detest the inconveniences that corruption introduces into their lives but, as individuals, very few people are averse to making money through a deal, as long as nobody exposes them.

Acknowledgement of this contradiction is part of what the public appreciates in Wainaina's humorous indictment of the situation in Kenya. Another part of the song's appeal is that it makes people laugh through its witty use of different slang-words for corruption. During one concert, Wainaina threw out handfuls of tea bags, much to the delight of the crowd. "Chai", or tea, is slang for a bribe. He sings:

"Ukitaka chai ewe ndugu nenda Limuru
(If you want tea [bribe], brother, go to Limuru)[13]

In another lyric, he advises:

"Ukitaka soda ewe Inspekta burudika na Fanta
(If you need a soda [bribe], Police Inspector, refresh yourself with a Fanta)."

The song's message annoyed the government and, although the independent radio stations continued playing the number regularly, it was denied airtime on state-run broadcasters. At a music festival, attended by the then Kenyan Vice-President, George Saitoti, the organisers tried to stop Wainaina from performing *Kitu Kidogo*. Only after an outcry from the audience, did the band perform the song. Wainaina says, 'My thought process was: I'm not going to stop because a couple of people are going to be angered by this. I had the vice-president in front of me, and it's important that this message gets across'[14].

On a positive note, however, although ending corruption still has a long way to go, *Nchi ya Kitu Kidogo* would have struggled to get radio airtime, or be sold publicly in shops a decade before. But, as multi-party politics and related democratic practices have begun to take hold, the culture of fear and suppression in Kenya has receded. Young Kenyans like Eric Wainaina are using their newfound freedom, to try to change the bad, old ways of their leaders and the citizenry.

Under this kind of patriotism, citizens who support a particular governmental action as well as those who oppose it are all behaving patriotically because they have reached an independent, albeit different, decision about what course of action is in the best interest of the country.

Conclusion

This overview of the relationship between music and politics in Kenya through the past half century reveals that music has indeed, functioned as a primary site of contestation of power. In reaction to state oppression, including censorship and overt propaganda, musicians have over and again played a privileged role in offering alternative narratives because of their access to a political platform. Counter-cultures arose that thrived in spite of the occasional if sometimes repressive censorship measures that were used to silence them. Popular songs produced away from the eyes of officialdom provided spaces within which people could not only experience moments of freedom, but could also construct their own regimes of truth and meaning in the music. Ultimately, these alternate regimes of truth amounted to contesting narratives of official patriotism: definitions of what acting in the interests of the nation consists. Usually, variations of what patriotism constitutes abound when leaders are perceived as acting against their subjects. Kenyan musicians have not, however, always retained the moral high ground in the eyes of the people. Indeed many have been accused of propping up despotic regimes by performing patriotic praise songs for authoritarian regimes. Accused of sycophancy for the sake of personal aggrandizement, or to increase their individual access to power and money, such musicians reply that their motives were economic not political and that they only perform what many people wish to hear. This argument surfaces the fundamental conflicts that emerge around the complex transactions that occur at the intersections between money and power.

Musicians have constantly needed to negotiate the conflicts and congruencies between the political power effected through voicing the interests of rulers, or those of the nation's subjects and the economic benefits of doing so, gained either from hand-outs or through accessing the mass market. Whatever their actions, however, they seem ultimately to be judged according to the moral expectations of a traditional praise poet: that they use their privileged access to a platform appropriately, that is, to raise their voices for the common good.

Joseph Kamaru is one Gĩkũyũ musician who has combined the power of both praise and protest in his music spanning for over five decades, over different ruling regimes. A close analysis of Kamaru and his adept use of the Gĩkũyũ language while straddling between being a thorn in the government's flesh and a collaborator constitutes the basis of the following chapter.

Notes

[1] These songs were genres of Gĩkũyũ music that predated the Mau Mau but were customized to the revolutionary era during the struggle for independence. To call them Mau Mau songs as wa Kinyatti does, denies them their roots, since there were Gĩkũyũ songs of resistance even before the Mau Mau. I view them in this research as songs sang in support of the Mau Mau, during the period.

[2] Ogude quotes *Pole Pole Mzee* (Deepest Sympathy, Grand Old Man), by Isaya Mwinamo (1963) and *Kenyatta Aliteswa Sana* (Kenyatta was Tortured so Much), by John Mwale in the same year.

[3] This song was released immediately after the 1982 attempted *coup d'etat* and was continually played on the national broadcaster for a long period as the then president dealt with the shock of the insurgency.

[4] This refers to Kenneth Matiba and Charles Rubia, who were detained in 1990 during the agitation for multi-party democracy in Kenya, after they insisted on holding a public meeting at the historic Kamukunji grounds in Nairobi. Although the struggle for democracy started long before that, their Gĩkũyũ followers see them as vanguards in the eventual re-introduction of multi-party politics in Kenya.

[5] Sammy Wambua. 'Songsters Outdid Themselves in their Rush to Praise the President's Regime', in *The Daily Nation*, December 24th, 2002, p.13.

[6] This practice had antecedents during the Kenyan struggle for independence when many Christian songs were altered to praise the freedom fighters.

[7] Pugliese, (1993:24) notes that 'Biblical analogies were often used to convey messages. For instance, Kenyatta was referred to as 'the shepherd of black people ... and as God's instrument for the salvation of the Gĩkũyũ since ''He was given the rod of leadership from God like Moses in Egypt''. Songs in praise of Gĩkũyũ colonial chiefs were fairly

common in the 1930s. In the 1940s, new songs were composed to pay tribute to the Gĩkũyũ politicians who were fighting against the colonial government'.

[8] It is important to note at this point that the praise genre amongst the pre-colonial Gĩkũyũ society was in existence. Such were songs that honoured various individuals or age groups for heroic performances. I have in mind heroes like Wang'ombe wa Ihira who was renowned for his bravery after he killed a leopard single handedly. The 1920s saw the rise of anti-colonial efforts best exemplified by the arrest of Harry Thuku in 1922 by the colonial government. The popular *Kanyegenyũri* signaled the first Gĩkũyũ political song in colonial times. *Kanyegenyũri*' was composed to commemorate the bravery of the Gĩkũyũ women who protested against the arrest of Thuku. Another famous political song genre, the *Mũthĩrĩgũ* appeared during the 1929 female circumcision controversy and was banned in January 1930'. (Pugliese, 1993:16)

[9] John Kariuki. 'Flashback to Praise Songs Era', in the *Sunday Nation*, 3 November, 2002, Lifestyle, p vii.

[10] The music awards in sub-Saharan Africa are named after the *Kora*, a 21-string bridge-harp used extensively in West Africa

[11] The State run media found itself in a dilemma when the same song they denied airtime was nominated for the annual KORA Awards. This left them with no option but to air the song as it now had an international recognition.

[12] The anti-graft watchdog Transparency International, put Kenya in the top five most corrupt countries in the world in 2000 and was rated 84th out of 90 countries in the body's 2001 Corruption Perceptions Index. The launch was held in Berlin on the 28 August 2002 where Kenya again dominated in the top ten ranks of the most corrupt nations in the world. www.transparency.org.

[13] Limuru is a major tea growing area in Kenya

[14] Eric Wainaina in an interview with Ishbel Matheson, on BBC.

CHAPTER FOUR

Joseph Kamaru's Music: Cutting with *Words*, not *Swords*

While discussing Gĩkũyũ popular music in postcolonial Kenya, a detailed study of musician Joseph Kamaru is almost unavoidable. Through an analysis of his songs, which touch on most facets of everyday life in Kenya, Kamaru also demonstrates how popular songs are webs of ambiguity, which can support widely divergent readings. As Hofmeyr (2004:131) argues, 'the careers of popular musicians will often traverse almost absurdly different positions as performers, chameleon-like, improvise around and explore and indeed dramatize the chaotic plurality of the postcolony'. Kamaru accomplishes this role, especially through his adept use and knowledge of the Gĩkũyũ language and traditions in his songs. This chapter explores the ambiguity of the musician alongside the contradictions of the postcolonial Kenya state. Cutting with words in this context implies Kamaru's penchant for not mincing words, and the use of words, proverbs and metaphors from the Gĩkũyũ cultural repertoire, while offering a third degree of the politics of the day.

While analysing the songs of Joseph Kamaru, this chapter focuses on the ambiguity of the musician throughout the changing faces of politics in Kenya. Of major interest, therefore, is the musician's use of language and metaphors, and appropriation of the rich repertoire of Gĩkũyũ customs and traditions, which are avenues through which he aptly captures the ambivalences, and contradictions of postcolonial Kenya. Kamaru's songs, as will be seen later bring to the fore issues of identity (class, ethnic groups and communities as well as ethnicities). These songs thus, are 'representing facets of outlooks, practices and experiences in a world which has ambivalences and contradictions' Gecau (1993:151). While analysing his songs, this chapter treats them as texts. Text, according to Hanks (1989:95) can be taken 'heuristically to designate any configuration of signs that is coherently interpretable by some community of users'. In this same vein, Fairclough (1992:4) defines texts to refer to 'any product of social interaction, whether spoken or written'. In light of the above, the common denominator is the social element of texts, which in view of this chapter, is Kamaru's songs. Notes Kwaramba (1997:15):

> Texts are not studied as mere end products of literary creativity, but as both end products of social processes and also as potential vehicles for shaping and reshaping these social processes.

She adds that there exists a relationship between language, power and ideology. This chapter treats Kamaru's music and his use of language as both a product and resource in shaping social relationships. After introducing Kamaru, the chapter looks at his creative efforts during the two ruling regimes of Jomo Kenyatta and Daniel arap Moi. It becomes crucial, when analysing these songs to fully understand the prevailing circumstances surrounding the production of the song and the singer. This chapter interprets the song texts, not independent of the extra-textual world.

Kamaru the musician

Joseph Kamaru Macharia, or Kamaru wa Wanjiru, as he is popularly known is a celebrated Gĩkũyũ musician with over 3,000 compositions to his credit. Kamaru has been on the music scene since 1966. His music borrows heavily from the traditional genres like '*Mũthũngũci, Njũkia, Mwomboko, Ngũchũ, Mũũmbũro* and *Mũthĩrĩgũ*, but also adopts other styles such as Reggae, Calypso, Rumba and the local Benga'[1]. Through a skilful use of the Gĩkũyũ language, tradition and customs, Kamaru's songs have always produced lively commentaries on the everyday social and political issues in Kenya, an attribute that has contributed greatly to his popularity.

Kamaru, to a large extent, forms the epicentre of Gĩkũyũ music in the 60s and 70s during President Kenyatta's reign. Kamaru has been making hit records since 1967 when he released hit song *Celina*. While there were other popular musicians at the same period, but who were concerned with other themes, like relationships, culture, urbanisation, religion and traditions, Kamaru seemed to be the only Gĩkũyũ musician who had the courage to use his music to comment on politics. He sees himself as a 'teacher, expressing the traditional values of his culture, as well as contemporary social comment'[2].

Kamaru sees the role of the musician in the society as the custodian of the community's culture. In most of his songs, he commits his lyrics to enlightening his audience about the Gĩkũyũ culture. In the song, *Mĩtugo ya Agĩkũyũ*, (The Customs of the Gĩkũyũ he teaches the audience about the most important aspects of the Gĩkũyũ culture, tradition and customs. Listening to the song would seem like a summary of Kenyatta's *Facing Mt Kenya* (1938),³ where stanza by stanza, he gives out the names Gĩkũyũ clans, the traditional setting of the Gĩkũyũ house, the various ceremonies of the community, the different generations, how meat was shared along gender and age brackets as well as the various traditional dances and dresses.

Latent in these lyrics, however, is an ingenious call for the Gĩkũyũ people to unite against any adversity. In one song, *Nĩ Maitho Tunĩĩte* (We are just turning a blind eye), literally meaning 'we know what we are doing', or 'we are just patient, but we know what is going on' he starts by a question:

> *Thuraku cingĩonekire hakuhĩ na nyũmbarĩ, andũ mekaga atĩa?*
> When safari ants were seen near your house, what did we use to do?

He replies in the next line:

> *Twathiũrũrũkagĩria nyũmba na mũhu*
> We would pour hot ash around our houses. (To keep them away)

Then he goes on:

> *Nĩtũkĩharĩrie mũhu tondũ mũndũ ũrĩ harĩa rũgũrũ nĩaretotora*
> Then let us keep the ash ready, because this man in the west is bragging.

This song was produced in 1983 when Moi, the then president decided to ban all tribal associations to consolidate his power. It was felt that the ban was particularly directed towards GEMA, Gĩkũyũ, Embu, Meru Association) a strong association bringing the three communities⁴ around Mount Kenya region together. Kamaru, in the same song advices the people that, *Kĩrĩnyaga nĩ ĩmwe* (All people around Mt. Kenya, are one people), and tells them to make sacrifices to God of Kirinyaga, so that, *mbĩa ĩrũmũkie nganangi* (the rat to let loose the straps of the basket). He further warns that *'Nĩ maitho tunĩĩte, njũkĩ cingiuma mwatũ, nĩkũrĩ ũngĩrutwo rũboora'*, (we are just patient; if the bees come out of the hive, somebody will be stung). Kamaru reminds the community of their past experiences in a very telling proverb:

Ngui ĩtoĩ ngarĩ, ndĩkũnjaga matũ, ĩhiũragia gĩcuthĩ yeterere gĩkuũ
A dog that does not know a leopard won't run away, it will just wag its tail waiting for death.

Such is an instance of Kamaru's skilful application of the Gĩkũyũ language, in a way that when suppression of freedom of expression was at its zenith in Kenya, this song escaped the censor's eyes. The linguistic ambiguity, where a song can have several meanings, is the hallmark of Kamaru's music. Prior to this song, songs he composed during periods of national crisis, as will be seen below were more explicit.

His most critical songs were composed during times of political crisis. In 1969, for instance, he composed a song defending President Kenyatta regarding allegations that he was involved in the assassination of trade unionist MP Tom Mboya. The Mboya murder created serious ethnic tensions between the Gĩkũyũ and the Luo, Kenya's two major ethnic groups.[5] But Kamaru was to make a turn-around six years later when populist MP Josiah Mwangi Kariuki's (popularly known as JM) mutilated body was found in Ngong Forest in the outskirts of Nairobi. Many accusing fingers were again pointed at the government. When Kamaru released his song, *J.M Mwendwo nĩirĩ* (J.M, The People's Hero) it was banned by the government. Kamaru had called for the arrest and prosecution of the killers (although, not confirmed hitherto, the hand of Jomo Kenyatta's government is very clear in the murder). D.K Kamau, another well-known musician also composed a song castigating the government over Kariuki's murder. However, after Kenyatta's death, the same Joseph Kamaru, whose 1975 song had been banned released a song, *Musa wa Andũ Airũ* (The Black People's Moses), that drew an analogy between the Biblical Moses and Kenyatta.

As Haugerud (1995:32) comments, theatre and music invoke polyvalent symbols that may inspire contradictory political actions. Thus, cultural productions as this chapter argues always reflect a competition for moral authority in the contemporary political struggles. The argument is anchored in the understanding that a national political culture is a 'loose collection of shifting meanings that are multiply-authored and context dependent. It is the outcome of a constant process of culture production' (Haugerud 1995: 103).

The chapter analyses several songs produced during important periods in the history of Kenya. Kamaru's music in the 60s was mostly love songs, as his hit song *Celina* depicts. This is the song, which shot him into the limelight of Kenyan music. It should be noted that prior to this, he had released a song, *Ūthoni wa Mbathi-inī*, still a song which heavily touched on relationships. Over the years though, Kamaru's songs touched on various themes; culture and tradition, history, politics and of late, he has made a complete turn around and records gospel songs. Spanning over four decades now, Kamaru has earned titles from scholars of his music; Douglass Paterson (1999) refers to him as the 'King of Kikuyu pop'; Gicingiri Ndigirigi refers to him as the 'teacher of the masses', (1994: 123) while listeners of his music have seen him as a 'prophet'. Issues he sings about actually come to pass, as will be discussed later in the chapter.

Kamaru's music during Kenyatta's years

Jomo Kenyatta, Kenya's first president reigned from 1963 when Kenya attained independence till his death in 1978. During these years, this chapter probes how Kamaru's music goes hand in hand with historical events in Kenya. As seen above, Kamaru's song in 1969 after the assassination of Tom Joseph Mboya was in clear support of the government of the day. Though the colonial legacy is apportioned much of the blame in most political crisis in Africa, Kenya's political problems and cracks in the nation, really intensified in 1969. Several events happened then. This was the year that the second general elections in Kenya were held. The only opposition party then, KPU (Kenya's People Union) was banned and its *de facto* leader Jaramogi Oginga Odinga sent into incarceration. Ethnic tensions between the Gīkūyū and the Luo flared up, and Kenyatta's visit in Kisumu (which was seen then as bedrock of opposition to Kenyatta's rule) was marred with violence. This is the context that shaped Kamaru's song, *Arooma Ka* (May he be stiff dead). In the song, Kamaru's rebuffs at those people who were claiming that

Kenyatta was too old to rule. He duly warns those that were against Kenyatta's rule:

Arooma ka - May he be stiff dead
Aroitīka - may he wither
na mahūri make - and his lungs
makarīrwo Kīrīnyaga - will be eaten on Mount Kenya
nī tūihū twa mīrūngarū - by mongooses.
Jogoo ya KANU –KANU's cockerel (the symbol of the party)
Nīyo īkwambata igūrū - will forever be hoisted high!

Kamaru, in his song tries to show Kenyatta's popularity from Mombasa to Kisumu, from Ngong to Karimatura (GarbaTulla). The mention of Ngong here is significant as will be seen later.

Despite commenting on the politics of the day and voicing his support for the ruling party, Kamaru also points out to the predator-prey relationship that characterised the tensions between the ruling elite. Drawing on the metaphor of the mongoose, the ambiguity comes out clear given that the cockerel was and still is the symbol of the party KANU. Mongooses are the greatest threat of a poultry farmer. They are known to feed on a large number of chicken when they strike. The implication here though is that Kenyatta is the main cockerel, those opposing him are either hens, or young chicken that are more prone to mongoose attacks. The mongoose metaphor also implies that all Kenyans were chicken, under one rule of the cockerel, and the ideal punishment was to throw them to mongooses, the most common threat to chicken The mention of Mount Kenya, the mythical abode of Ngai, the god of the Gīkūyū community gives ethnic connotations to the song.

Kenyatta's statement in a speech made in 1975 more or less reiterated the same. Faced with dissent and opposition from his government after the grisly murder of populist MP, Josiah Mwangi Kariuki as seen in the next example, and the attempted cover-up, he sternly warned: 'the hawk is in the sky. It is ready to descend on chickens who stray from the pathway', (Miller, 1984: 53). Within a few days, opposition waned but the crisis of Kariuki's death haunted him until his death in 1978.

1972 marked yet another suspicious death of a prominent politician, Ronald Ngala, under mysterious circumstances, which have not been unravelled up to this moment. However, Kamaru didn't release a song in 1972 until much later in 1975 when another famous politician died. In this year, a former Mau Mau detainee and a populist Member of Parliament, J.M Kariuki, popularly known as JM was found murdered in Ngong Forest with his body mutilated. He is said to have been one of the prominent politicians who fronted the case of the landless and squatters in Kenya. He was critical of the government's policy to resell land to the colonial settlers whereas most Kenyans remained landless. Kenyatta was not amused by his vocal criticism. His death was seen by many as a sign to silence him forever. The question most people would have raised would be what Kamaru would release next. He never repeated the mistake he made in 1969. This time, he released a song that was quite critical of the government:

> *Thirikari tondū Kariūki nīakua* - authorities, now that Kariuki is dead
> *Arutītwo magego na maitho* - with his teeth removed, his eyes gouged out
> *Na tikūiya kana kūragana* - and he wasn't a thief or a murderer
> *Thakame ndīgaitīke nīūndū wake* - let's not shed more blood
> *Rekei Ngai arute wīra wake* - let God do His work

The song not only describes the grisly murder, but also questions the government to provide the answers to the death of an innocent man. The song somehow contradicts his earlier song, where he prophesies doom to whoever was critical to Kenyatta's rule. Whereas mongooses on Mount Kenya did not eat Kariuki's body, it was mutilated and left to the hyenas in Ngong forest! Ngong is earlier mentioned in the 1969 song. Prophet Kamaru?

The irritating verse that was critical and might have led to the banning of the song predicted doom again to whoever was involved in the murder:

> *Mūmūtinia ciīga ciothe cia mwīrī* - whoever mutilated his body
> *Mūmūtwari mūhara-inī wa nyamū* - whoever took him to the wild animals
> *No nginya akagaragario na mwatū* - will be rolled in a beehive
> *Mūingī wothe wa Kenya wīroreire* - with the Kenyan public watching.

Kamaru invokes Gīkūyū customs to send home a message. Criminals in pre-colonial Gīkūyū society would be rolled downhill in a beehive as a means of punishment, Wanjohi, (1997:216). Though the government denied responsibility, all indications pointed to a heavy hand in government involvement. In parliament, when asked to explain the whereabouts of the MP, the then VP, Daniel arap Moi (who was later to become president) blatantly lied to the House that Hon. Kariuki was on a business trip to Zambia. Later on, a parliamentary select committee also implicated the government. Kamaru's song was banned on the only national broadcaster; Voice of Kenya (VOK).[6]

The death of Kariuki, a Gĩkũyũ led to an internal split among the Gĩkũyũ ethnic group[7], alongside a revolt against the government in parliament, Miller (1984: 52). Kamaru's turn-around from the 1969 political crisis after Tom Mboya's murder could be interpreted thus. This is an issue I pick up later when I consider the audience. Having heavily castigated the government and by extension the president for Kariuki's murder, two important events happened in 1978, in relation to Kamaru's music.

On the morning of August 22nd 1978, Kenya's first president, Jomo Kenyatta died in Mombasa State House. A high profile delegation alongside thousands of mourning Kenyans witnessed his state funeral. His casket draped in the national flag of Kenya was paraded along the streets of Nairobi on horse carriage. Kamaru's prophecy had come to pass: the murderer of JM Kariuki was finally being rolled in a bee-hive[8] to the full glare of not only Kenyans, but the world at large. It is at this point that Kamaru's songs were taken seriously, and the prophet tag attached to him.

Ironically, at the time of mourning, Kamaru was at it again. This time, he released a song praising the late president, christening him the Moses of the Black People in his song, *Musa wa Andũ Airũ*, a reference to Biblical Moses' efforts to rescue the Israelites from Egyptian's slavery. Within the Gĩkũyũ traditions, one does not quarrel with the dead. The Gĩkũyũ people 'believe that the spirits of the dead, like living human beings, can be pleased or displeased by the behaviour of an individual or family group, or an age group' (Kenyatta, 1938: 266)

The vacillating nature of Kamaru is what this chapter points at. As Bogumil Jewsiewicki (1997:440), argues:

> Often of populist inspiration, research on popular culture emphasises the political critique, the subversive character of the text. Yet it

must be admitted that at least as often, songs praise the incumbent regime, conveying its values and transmitting its structure.

That Kamaru both praised and criticised the incumbent and his regime places the artist fully within a role commonly expected of musicians all over the African continent – that of the praise poet (South African) or *griot* (West Africa). Tradition has it that a musician recognised as fulfilling this function is duty bound to publicly highlight both the positive attributes and failings of a leader.

In view of the understanding that relationships in a postcolony are based on mutual zombification, as Mbembe argues, one can argue here, in case of Kamaru, that popular arts, in this instance, popular music, not only are affected by the socio-political realities of the day, but they do affect them as well. The futuristic predictions of Kamaru, as in the song on JM, clearly point this out. It is Karin Barber's (1987:1-2) point that buttresses this argument:

> Popular arts penetrate and are penetrated by political, economic and religious institutions in ways that may not always be predictable from our own experiences.

Suffice it to say that most Kamaru's songs, outlive the event, and have been or can be appreciated, not because of their aesthetic value, but on their relevance to the Kenyan history. This is what gives them an independent life. Among the oral interviews conducted during this study, mostly among elderly Gĩkũyũ people, there is always a reference to Kamaru's songs when responding to issues around politics in Kenya.

The Moi era

In 1982, the government of Daniel arap Moi, the successor of Jomo Kenyatta, faced an insurgent from the army. Though the coup was quashed, loss of life and property was rampant, and the politics of the day assumed a completely new dimension. Most of Moi's trusted aides were implicated in the coup and for those who survived jail sentences had to contend with their political lives in limbo. Kamaru's response couched in linguistic ambiguity was in his song, *Chunga Marima* (Watch your Steps).

Chunga marima - watch your steps
Ūkīgūa ndūkagūe na niī - if you fall down, you'll all be by yourself
Chunga marima - watch your steps
Na ndūkanoige ndiakwīrire - don't say I never warned you
Chunga marima – watch your steps

Chunga Marima dwelt on the politics of the day. The former Attorney General, and the then Minister for Constitutional affairs, Charles Njonjo, was accused by fellow politicians of being behind the attempted coup of 1982[9].He was branded a 'traitor' and Kamaru joined in with his song to castigate him:

Huko nī cietherwo itatī ikwa itanathira - Let get traps for the moles before they finish our yams
Ciarema ciīkīrwo maaī - if we cannot trap them, let us pour water in their holes
Mwendia būrūri, nīahītwo - the sellout in our country should be hunted down
Atanabuīria - Before he disappears

In the context, the song was a clear support of the government of the day against those who dared raise a finger against it. As a means of consolidating power, president Moi encouraged a cult of hero-worship:

Besides being the commander-in-chief of the armed forces, head of state and government and the chancellor of all public universities, the president acquired some other titles such as the 'prince of peace', 'number one farmer', 'the chief conservationist', etc. several institutions and places were named after the president and a culture of hero-worshipping permeated the country's body politic. Sycophancy became the hallmark of the Moi one-party state. (Schmidt and Kibara, 2002: 8)

Kamaru's music would easily have fallen in this cycle of sycophancy. The President appreciated the power of music as a propaganda tool and he used it to the fullest.

The song *Chunga Marima* appears in Kamaru's Album, Kenyan Patriotic Songs, Vol 1. Vol 2 appears under the title, *Ūrathi wa Kamarū* (Kamaru's prophecy), released in 1983. Kamaru, however, deconstructs himself. In one song, *Ndeto Irĩ Na Ene* (Stories have their tellers), he clearly says that his songs are not political and that his trade is just a means of eking out a living:

Mareenda ndigacoke kũina - They want me to stop singing
Na rĩngĩ ndinagĩra kwenda - And probably, I don't just sing
Nĩnyone gacati ga gwĩkĩra - I want to be able to buy a new shirt
Kamarũ, mwaria njarie - I Kamaru, I only say what's been said
Ngũkua kĩ? - Why pick a fight with me?

Given that his music is purely in the Gĩkũyũ language, we can argue that his narration of history of Kenya is as far as it suits his listeners. He constantly reminds the Gĩkũyũ community to unite against any adversity. In the 1980s, Moi banned all tribal associations with a view of consolidating power. So can one say that Kamaru's is Gĩkũyũ's history, as opposed to that of Kenya? Kamaru brings us to the idea of the contending narrations of nationhood and struggles over citizenship.

Kamaru's popularity in line with a wide audience across ethnic barriers points to the weakness of such an argument above. Notes Keith Negus (1994:121):

Once in circulation, music and other cultural forms cannot remain bounded in any one group and interpreted simply as an expression that speaks to or reflects the lives of that exclusive group of people.

The suspicious deaths of Tom Mboya, J.M Kariuki, the 1982 short-lived coup and the disillusionment with different ruling regimes were not events that only affected the Gĩkũyũ community. Again, it doesn't really matter even if his music appealed to a Gĩkũyũ audience. As long as oppression, anti-democratic and unpopular nuances by any government are practiced, popular music will continue to have a resonance as a signifier of a culture created out of these experiences. The argument that Kamaru only appeals to a Gĩkũyũ audience ignores the significant ideological, political and class differences within the community. Kamaru's song, *Rĩrĩa Mũgũtwenja* (When you are oppressing us) points toward this direction.

Therefore, the argument that his music is in some way expressing the unity of a particular group of people must continually confront the apparent disunities and differences that are there in the world. Talking of Kamaru's music across the different ruling regimes, thus, helps in understanding:

> under what conditions do particular musical codes, signs and symbols become used and claimed as expressions of particular social and cultural identities. The implication here is that music and other cultural forms are just as much part of the making of cultural identities - the process is not simply one way whereby some fixed identity leads to a particular type of music'. (Negus, 1994: 122).

The re-introduction of multi-party

With the repeal of the repressive Section 2A in the Kenyan constitution in 1991, which gave rise to the re-introduction of multi-party democracy, it can be rightly argued that freedom of expression received a major boost. Prior to this, Kamaru had released an album in 1990, *Mahoya ma Būrūri* (Prayers for the Nation) that was questioning the lack of clear rule of law by the government. Seen as contempt to the government, Kamaru was held for questioning by the authorities.[10] However, his *Ndūmīrīri Kūrī Mbeū Njīthī* (Message to the Youth) album in 1992, prior to the December multi-party general elections was a clear analysis of all the presidential candidates, taking a middle-ground stance. In the album, he emphasizes that it is only God who can give Kenya a proper and just leader. In an interview with researcher Gicingiri Ndigirigi (1994:132), he says that he didn't want to be associated with any political party or leader. This wasn't to be though. Notes Wekesa (2002:12):

> At the height of the campaign for the multiparty elections in 1992 ... Kamaru from the Kikuyu ethnic community was seen by the ruling party, KANU, as an important vehicle to deliver the Kikuyu votes. He would appear at [most] rallies in Central Province [the home of the Kikuyu] where he attracted and entertained thousands of people who would probably have had no other opportunity to watch him perform live. His recordings were constantly played on the national radio and television station, KBC.

In a public meeting however on October 20th 1992, a national day celebration, Kenyatta Day to honour the heroes of the Mau Mau struggle,

Kamaru told arap Moi, the then president of Kenya, and leader of KANU to his face that he was not the kind of leader Kenyans wanted. The strange bed relationship between him and the ruling party ended then.

In 1993 after the elections and eventual win to Daniel Moi, he produced an album, *Mũnyongoro* (The Millipede) advising the main losers, Kenneth Matiba of FORD (Forum for the Restoration of Democracy) Asili, Jaramogi Oginga Odinga of FORD Kenya, and Mwai Kibaki of DP (Democratic Party) amongst others to accept defeat for the sake of development of the country. He urged them to cooperate, now that the 'cock' had the 'millipede' in its grip. The use of these symbols is relevant given that KANU's symbol was and still is a cockerel. The song can be interpreted as a rejoinder, to the earlier scathing album, *Message to the Youth*.

Towards the end of 1993, he produced *Kũroga* (To Bewitch). In the song, he assumes a position on top of Mount Kenya (the mythical residence of Ngai, the God of the Gĩkũyũ, seeking advice from the deity. He appears to be bewitching all the leaders who led to the flare up of ethnic violence in the Burnt Forest and Molo regions in Kenya's Rift Valley province[11] and other areas. He curses[12] the leaders who have stashed money in foreign accounts and embezzled the taxpayers' money. The musician in the song condemns adulterers and warns that those he has not mentioned will be inflicted by the leprosy of the above curse. He advocates for a public meeting where the citizens would decide how they want to be governed, and threatens the government that its people will go to Molo and Burnt Forest to fight the perpetrators of ethnic violence. Goes a line:

The Mau Mau vanquished the colonialist;
We too can stop the perpetrators

In this song, which the singer talks in a background of instruments, he takes the position of a preacher, giving examples to buttress his message. Coincidentally, this was his last secular number for in April 1993, he converted to Christianity.

Kamaru, the convert[13]

For a musician who was known for political commentary, advocacy for Gĩkũyũ cultural revival and sometimes, lewd lyrics, like his album, Xrated *Adults Only*, his conversion to Christianity leaves questions worth answering in this chapter. In the years after 1997 especially, the political space was opened up, such that the government could condone dissenting voices. Before then, the public, unlike the artist, could not voice concerns about the way that they were ruled. The musician had an upper hand, in commenting on politics in music. With the entrenchment of democratic ideals like freedom of expression and association, anybody now could comfortably express discontent in different platforms and forum. The question then is whether musicians really say what they want the audience to hear, or whether it is a question of easier access to power and money. How the musicians tackle the new challenges is a question beyond the scope of this chapter and offers space for new research imperatives. Kamaru's change of religious status led him to producing gospel music, a trend he has continued hitherto. In an article tracking the lure of gospel music amongst many musicians in Kenya, Amos Ngaira (2002) argues:

> ... [T]he avenues for marketing and selling one's product are wider, from churches to open-air crusades to Christian TV and radio stations over and above the normal secular fora. Lure of vernacular renditions, too, is helping boost sales, with many artistes releasing replica copies in Kiswahili and local languages.

Probably, this accounts for Kamaru's switch to gospel music. As said earlier, this is not a topic this chapter intends to deal with at this moment. However, a crucial analysis of Kamaru's audience is necessary.

Kamaru's audience

Most of his songs are purely in the Gĩkũyũ language. His music, however, requires a critical appreciation. The music is deeply rooted in the Gĩkũyũ oral tradition. The fact that his music spanning over four decades is readily available in music shops in Kenya denotes a wide audience. Linguistic ambiguity is one of the cornerstones of Kamaru's music. His late 1980s release, conveniently named *Adults Only* was loaded with sexual innuendos and bawdy lyrics. The songs became quite popular, but it was only those armed with the proficiency of the language who could understand the lyrics.

Kamaru's use of proverbs especially in most of his songs as well as the linguistic ambiguity sends out messages to his audience, but who are subject to interpreting the proverbs differently. By use of proverbs, the popularity of Kamaru's music derive from the fact that they are presented in a language and a discursive medium that renders them more available for criticism and discussion. For instance, his song *Chunga Marima* can be read from two levels, once we appreciate the several proverbs therein. The song apparently was a castigation of the dissenters of Moi's rule, as we have seen above. On a cautionary note though, Kamaru is giving advice to politicians:

Mwaka wa hiti ndūhoyanagīrwo rigī
When hyenas are in abundance, one doesn't beg a wicker-work door.[14]

Signifying the jungle that politics is, Kamaru applies this proverb, which is normally used for counselling, moderation and prudence in generosity. That Moi's trusted aides betrayed him by planning the coup in 1982, the proverb extends help to the besieged, that in politics, it's all about your survival first.

The proverb, however, derives a lot from the lives of the pre-colonial Gīkūyū people. Living in animal infested areas, hyenas would at some seasons wreak havoc by attacking people in their homes. The wicker-work door, a kind of a gate outside and around the hut could easily prevent the marauding animals from reaching your home. Since all people would be affected, this won't be the right time to lend it or borrow the door from your neighbour. Drawing from Gīkūyū oral tradition points at crucial observations when discussing Kamaru's audience: Wekesa (2002:9) argues:

> People's sense of themselves always come from the use of images, symbols and a wide series of responses which they come to identify with, and which also distinguish them from others.

Given the 1982 context of the song then, the above proverb again can be read as a warning to the Gīkūyū community, that they should be self-reliant, especially in politics. Kamaru's vacillation and middle-ground stance is manifest once again.

In the same song he uses a host of other proverbs which, when analysed would reveal this ambiguity. For instance;

Njoya cia njamba ticio cia mwera
The feathers of a cock are different from those of a hen.
Mũikia ndoĩ mwehereri
Whoever is throwing a missile doesn't know where it will land.

The first proverb above again mentions the metaphor of the cockerel and the hen, discussed earlier in the chapter but also shows the relationships between the rulers and the ruled, or the differences between the ruling elite.

Just like readers in works of fiction, the audience in music grasps essential features of these proverbs and uses them to interpret their own social experience. As Karin Barber (1997:357) argues, 'proverbs meaning is never complete until they are applied to a concrete situation'. Therefore, one can argue that a similar proverb can be applied to different situations. The argument here is that though Kamaru's songs were recorded years ago, the use of proverbs makes them relevant presently in discussing Kenya's changing politics. The concerns with the everyday life, be it social or political, has made Kamaru's music appeal to a wide audience across different ages of people born in different periods of Kenya's political history.

Following his conversion to Christianity in 1993, Kamaru's secular music has enjoyed a greater revival, especially with *Mũgithi* artists with their renditions of his songs, and with the proliferation of vernacular radio stations, an indication of Kamaru's popularity in the Kenyan music scene.

Conclusion

> What do you think an artist is? An imbecile who has only his eyes if he is a painter, or ears if he's musician or a lyre at every level if he is a poet, or even, if he's a boxer, just his muscles? On the contrary, he's at the same time a political being, constantly alive to heartrending, fiery or happy events, to which he responds in every way. Pablo Picasso, quoted in Dore Ashton (1972:149)

The overview of Kamaru the musician in this chapter tends to point at the role of the artist in narrating the history of the nation as well as providing political commentaries. More importantly is the use of language to drive his message home. Metaphoric expressions and allusions leave the audience (whether the government or the citizen) with a license on how to interpret the songs. Couching his music however in the extra-textual (the real happenings in the country) leads one to a conclusion in line with David Harker's (1985:76) position, that, 'unless we locate cultural products in history, we cannot hope to understand culture'. Kamaru's use of deep language and metaphors clearly depict the ambiguous nature the musician operated in. The ambiguity here can be used to highlight how the musician 'expresses the hidden transcript of the ordinary people especially in the 1980s when, because of the political situation, the message was forced to remain implicit' (Gecau, 1997:154).

Seen as a constant threat by the authorities because of a wide audience, Kamaru's vacillating nature over the years was a strategy to cushion him against the wrath of the government. Again, this explains the complex relationship between the rulers and the ruled in postcolonial Kenya. Whereas the musician may claim to be apolitical, it is clear from the analysis of the lyrics that the politics of the day dominate. Whether it's a comment or criticism of the ordinary man or the leader, loud political overtones cannot be ignored. Alongside politics, this chapter has also shown that Kamaru's music can be appreciated as a template for re-reading the history of the nation. Thirdly, music is seen in the chapter as a source of oral tradition, following Kamaru's use of the rich repertoire of the Gĩkũyũ traditions. The politics of production of music is manifest in analysing Kamaru and his music. The recourse to gospel music after the introduction of multiparty democracy is a search of identity amidst changing political atmosphere. Secondly, gospel music appears to be fetching more money than secular music in Kenya. The bottom line, however, is that the musician in his trade has epitomized the role of the artist in the society, as Pablo Picasso's quote above elucidates. To paraphrase John Street (1997:14), music affords an opportunity for people to enjoy and articulate their political feelings. From the pleasures of popular music, people become engaged with politics through the feelings it articulates, the identity it offers, the passions it elicits and the responses it prompts. Music and politics therefore exist alongside each other. From the Gĩkũyũ oral tradition, this chapter concludes with a proverb: *Gũtema na kanua ti gũtema na rũhiũ* [To cut with the tongue (or words) is different from cutting with the sword].

The postcolony in Africa is comprised of different and shifting identities. While Kamaru, representing the old generation of musicians in Kenya borrows heavily from the Gīkūyū oral tradition, a new breed of musicians has sprouted, especially in the 1990s, whose main contribution, especially in the study of identities is to blur the perceived boundaries; ethnic/national, rural/urban, sacred/profane, moral/amoral and traditional/modern. The next chapter concerns itself with the play on urban/rural identities.

Notes

[1] Maina Mutonya et al., *Retracing Kikuyu Popular Music*. Ketebul Music. 2010. p. 25

[2] See Doug Paterson's 'The Life and Times of Kenyan Pop' in *World Music: The Rough Guide*, 1999.

[3] Jomo Kenyatta's *Facing Mount Kenya (*1938) is an ethnographic and anthropological study of the customs, culture, history and the general life of the pre-colonial Gīkūyū people. Kenyatta, himself from the community went on to become Kenya's first president after independence from the British in December 12th 1963.

[4] The languages of these three communities are mutually intelligible, and based on their geographical proximity; they regard themselves as cousins, and have shared a political bond for a long time.

[5] After the assassination of Tom Mboya in 1969, there was growing discontent as an accusing finger was pointed to the executive. With the instability looming, Kenyatta and his advisers started administering oaths to the Gīkūyū to cement tribal and political solidarity against their adversaries, mostly perceived to be the Luo community. At the oathing ceremonies, they swore that 'the flag of Kenya shall not leave the 'House of Mūmbi' (Ochieng and Ogot, 1995: 102 and Andrew Morton. 1998:160). The Gīkūyū people invoke the name of their mythical ancestors when the community feels threatened. Mumbi is revered as the mother of the tribe.

[6] Another musician, D.K. Kamau produced a song about the brutal murder of J.M. Kariuki. Some of the lyrics pointed to the popular belief that the murder was state-engineered. 'It is rumoured that the musician was summoned to Gatundu [Kenyatta's home] and thoroughly caned by the President, Jomo Kenyatta, which was the late President's preferred punishment for dissent even among his fellow politicians'. See www.enchanted-landscapes.com.

[7] A popular saying after Kariuki's murder was that 'the hyenas had eaten one of their own', meaning that the legislator suffered in the hands of his own people, the Gĩkũyũ. Again, worth noting is that Kariuki at one time served as Kenyatta's private secretary.

[8] The beehive here metaphorically constitutes Kenyatta's casket, and the parading of the casket along Nairobi streets could be read as the rolling of the bee-hive downhill.

[9] What came to be referred as 'The traitor affair' in 1983, months after the failed coup threw a complicated challenge to the country. Charles Njonjo, then the most feared minister Kenya had 'established an elaborate machinery involving the police, senior civil servants and the judiciary which provided him with a formidable power base' (Ogot and Ochieng': 1995:200). After being named the traitor, his power base was dismantled and left Moi's powers in Kenyan politics unchallenged

[10] When Kenyan authorities called Kamaru for questioning, he told them his cassette was patriotic. 'I tried to explain to them that I am praying to my people. I am praying to our leaders, praying for my country, so I don't see why you are trying to ban my cassette' (Haugerud, 1995:30)

[11] See Peter M Kagwanja. 'Facing Mount Kenya or Facing Mecca? The Mũngĩkĩ, Ethnic Violence and the Politics of the Moi Succession in Kenya 1987-2002'. *African Affairs* 102:25-49 January 2003.

[12] The Gĩkũyũ used to believe in the power of '*kĩrumi*', 'the curse'. Notes Kenyatta 1938:222, 'the fear of public opinion expressed in the way of curses was the chief preventative of mischief and crimes because there was no police organization in Gĩkũyũ society'. One of Kamaru's songs in the album is titled *Kĩrumi kĩa ũrĩ muoyo (The Curse of the Living)*, where he warns that the curse of the living is worse than the curse of the dead.

[13] In 2008, Kamaru made a comeback to secular music. Kamaru is perhaps the only Gĩkũyũ musician to have started out in secular performance, shifted to Gospel for 16 years and then moved back to secular music. Since December 2008, he has been composing a mix of secular and Gospel songs. To date, he has about 3,000 compositions to his name, in a career spanning over 45 years.

[14] Translation adopted from Gerald Joseph Wanjohi. *The Wisdom and Philosophy of African Proverbs: The Gĩkũyũ World-View.* Nairobi, 1997, p 165.

Joseph Kamaru, considered the father of the Kikuyu popular music in a live performance in Nairobi in December 2010 *(Photo by Maina Mūtonya)*.

Musician DK Kamau in action, December 2010. *(Photo by Maina Mūtonya)*

A modern version of *mwomboko*, a traditional dance of the Gīkūyū. Mwomboko was a kind of waltz for both men and women *(Photo by Maina Mūtonya)*.

The author with DK Kamau (left) one of the pioneer Kikuyu musicians since the 1970s.

A mūgithi performance during a graduation party. The participants are linked by holding on to the waist or shoulders of the one ahead. *Mūgithi* performance has come to define the ultimate entertainment in any social event amongst Kenyans. Recently, politicians have also adopted *mūgithi* in their political campaigns. *(Photo by Maina Mūtonya)*

Stetson hats and cowboy boots are a common feature of many a Gĩkũyũ musicians, that complete the picture of the Wild West, added to the western country rhythm that some of the musicians have adopted in their performances *(Photo by Maina Mũtonya)*.

Gĩkũyũ music has long been dominated by men. However, Queen Jane (center, in red beret) has for a long time, been one of the few female musicians until her death in June 2010 *(Photo by Maina Mũtonya)*.

A collection of Gĩkũyũ CDs *(Photo by Maina Mũtonya).*

Mount Kenya has been considered as the mythical abode of *Ngai*, the god of the Gĩkũyũ people. *(www.unep.org).*

Simba Centre, on Nairobi's downtown River Road, where many production and distribution houses for Gĩkũyũ music (both secular and gospel) are located *(Photo by Maina Mũtonya)*.

Musician Eric Wainaina with the author, December 2012.

An advertising page in a Kenyan newspaper preparing the readers for a fun-filled weekend (*Photo by Maina Mūtonya*).

CHAPTER FIVE

'Touch What You Don't Have': *Mūgithi[1]*, One-Man Guitar and Urban Identities

The 1990s marked an emergence of a relatively new genre in the Kenyan entertainment industry. The *Mūgithi* performance signaled a beginning of new directions largely in Kenyan music, and specifically Gīkūyū music in terms of themes and style. *Mūgithi*, in this chapter, is seen as a celebration of the city and sex. The performance, mostly an urban phenomenon dominated by Gīkūyū one-man guitarists, is discussed in this chapter as a major site for negotiation of identities and incorporates the interface and interplay between tradition and modernity,[2] especially so in the urban setting. The chapter begins by highlighting the inherent contradictions in creation and re-creation of urban identities as expressed in the music. The main argument here is that identities are always contested and different socio- economic situations call for a negotiation, if not a re-negotiation of identities.

Likewise, the chapter analyses the socio-economic conditions that led to the rise of this new genre, amidst the disillusionment in the 1990s that affected everyday life survival of the ordinary man, as seen in preceding chapters.

Urban identities, like all other identities are always contested terrains, especially with the knowledge that an argument for a fixed identity is always problematic. As Clark (2003: 3) contends, it is the popular cultural forms that are expressed in the urban landscape that provide an arena for engaging with and framing these complex debates around identity. In this light, the chapter investigates the performance of urban identities in the changing cultural terrains in music. The one-man guitar phenomenon and the resultant *Mūgithi* performance epitomize these concerns. How this music becomes vital in the performance and propagation of urban and sub-urban cultures and identities constitute engaging arguments as far as cosmopolitanism is concerned. Nairobi's sub-urban restaurants have provided a space for this musical blending of cultural influences that has produced so many innovative and distinctively Kenyan urban performance styles, *Mũgithi*. Similar to the *shebeen*[3] in a South African context, the restaurants located inside and outside the busy capital have necessitated the convivial interaction necessary for urban Kenyan social survival.[4]

Probably, owing to the informality that characterises this performance, there exists scanty literature on *Mũgithi* as a musical genre. Maupeu and Mbugua (2006) locate the bar as the space in which Gĩkũyũ nationalism thrived at the height of one party dictatorship of Daniel arapMoi (1978-2002) in the late 80s. This was mostly achieved through the performance of *Mũgithi*. Mutonya (2005; 2007) similarly locates the politics of everyday life through ethnic stereotypes as expressed in the music, while Githiora (2008) examines how the *Mũgithi* performance embodies *Gĩcaandĩ*, a Gĩkũyũ poetic tradition while recreating Gĩkũyũ traditions and social-cultural discourses.

The performance, referred to as 'one-man guitar' should in fact be labelled as a 'one-man, one-guitar', an expression that captures the reality of *Mũgithi*. The *Mũgithi* performance has, however, been borne of a guitar tradition that has defined the popular music of Kenya over the years. John Low (1982) has traced the history of the guitar music which has been present in the Kenyan music scene from as early as the 1900s. However, Low's research on the history of the Kenyan guitar styles is biased towards western Kenya, but coincidently which happens to be the ´home of so much fine Kenyan guitar music´ (1982:17). His assertion could be buttressed by the fact that even before the contact with foreign musical traditions the Luhya and Luo communities in Western Kenya had elaborate string instruments in such lyres as the Luo *nyatiti* and the Luhya´s *litungu*[5]. In fact, musicians from other parts of Kenya in the 60s who attempted the *benga*[6] beat had to hire guitarists from these two communities. For example, in the development of popular music of the Gĩkũyũ people, where *Mũgithi* performance falls into, and forms the mainstay of this article, one unforgettable name would be Odhiambo Sumba Rateng´´ (himself from western Kenya) who worked as a ´session guitarist on many Kikuyu songs with a variety of musicians for over thirty years´(Mutonya *et al*, 2010: 33).

With the appropriation of the guitar in Kenyan popular music, it is only subtle to assert in tandem with Doug Paterson (2000:509) that what is defining about Kenyan music is the interplay of guitars. Added to the existence of the traditional lyres, as explained above, the first contact with the guitar as it is known today was evident in Kenya ´even before 1900 when guitars were played among the freed slave´ (ibid). In the 50s and 60s, the guitar playing styles[7] in Kenya benefitted greatly from contacts with other parts of the world like Malawi, Zimbabwe, the then Zaire, South Africa, Latin America as well as America and Europe. Today, the Kenyan pop remains as this melange of musical styles that ´borrows freely and cross fertilise each other´ (Paterson, 509). The electrical guitar bands from the 60s hitherto have also thrived on this rich culture.

Presently, the Gĩkũyũ exhibit this 'cross-fertilization' especially from the western country music tradition, in terms of regalia and beats. Stetson hats and cowboy boots are a common feature of many a Gĩkũyũ musicians, that complete the picture of the Wild West, added to the western country rhythm that some o f the musicians have adopted in their performances.

Of relevance in this chapter is the fact that, although I dedicate my efforts to analysing an emergent one-man, one-guitar phenomenon known as *Mũgithi* in the 1990s, this tradition was vividly evident in the 1960s in Kenya. However, the slight difference was that while in the 60s, especially with the advent of the electric guitar which was louder and ´whose music could not be drowned by audience nose ... or swamped by singing and other instruments, therefore better to dance to´ (Low 1982: 27), the one-man guitarist was always accompanied by other band members playing different instruments, but the one-man guitarist from the 1990s onwards is all by himself/herself[8] as both the guitarist and the vocalist.

These performances now and then have been purely part and parcel of the urban culture. In the 60s, the songs of the Kenyan groups were aimed at the ´urban working class, whose *lingua franca* was Swahili´ (Low, 1982:29), although the richer Kenyans with higher aspirations tended to prefer Zairean or Western records. During this time, immediately after independence, the musicians had a conscious desire to develop a truly national music, hence the preoccupation with the Swahili language, which the independent nation had adopted as a national language.

While considering the *Mũgithi* spectacle of the 1990s, it is clear that the musicians are responding to the challenges of the Kenyan postcolony where the diverse cultures of the nation has been politicised, leading to a strong urge for Kenyans to identify more with their ethnic heritages, rather than as a nation. But as Coplan (1982: 125) argues, people in situations of urban change use musical metaphors as instruments for social movement, order and self-development. Musical performances ...help bring order out of the chaos of diverse and conflicting cultural images.

However, it is important to note that the emergence of *Mūgithi* also coincided with a period when Kenyans developed an affinity to their local music, which had been completely overwhelmed by Western music, as well as South African and Congolese beats. From the 1990s, Kenyans have evolved musical styles that consciously attempt to bring about a Kenyan rhythm. For example, the urban youth have *genge* and *kapuka*, styles that have a semblance to hip-hop and rap especially from the US, but with distinct local flavors. According to Nyairo (2004: 47):

> ...this fusion is not about how the local gets drawn and absorbed into Western modernity, but rather it is about the artful forging of local derivatives of modernity, a project that is clearly fraught with potential contradictions, and sometimes, given its techniques of appropriation, often lacks either consistency or cogency.

However, this is beyond the scope of this chapter. But as Githiora (2008: 92) argues, ´modern-day Kenyan musicians and especially *Mūgithi* and hip hop artists have either retained or continue to re-create traditional musical forms and practices by remaking modern music that is grounded in popular traditional forms´. It is against this background that this chapter turns its attention to the negotiation of urban identities in the performance of *Mūgithi* in Kenya.

The conceptualization and representation of urban identity is 'an enactment of the complex and multi-layered interweaving of culture, tradition ... gender and class' (Clark, 2003: 3). Thus, to paraphrase Brooks (1997), any discourse about identity and the politics of location holds the possibilities for the emergence of new and innovative sites of meaning and knowledge. The emergence of the *Mūgithi* phenomenon in the urban space of Kenya then assists in the performance of this interplay of divergent identities. Like most popular cultural forms and productions, *Mūgithi* becomes important in the discussion around the negotiation of urban identities because it straddles and dissolves distinctions. A study of this music then will provide insight into the manner in which old, new and fluid cultural identities emerge, are negotiated or contested within and between the spaces in urban areas where the music is performed.

Writing on the urbanisation of African music, Coplan asserts, the rich and varied associational life of most urban Africans 'has long included performance as a major focus of identity and cultural patterning' (1982: 115). The nucleus of the chapter in tandem, therefore, is to delineate the one-man-guitar phenomenon and the resultant *Mūgithi*, a musical trend emergent in the city of Nairobi, (Kenya) as a cultural site where urban identities are performed.

Like most urban centers, Nairobi is a cosmopolitan city housing people from the disparate ethnic, religious, class, gender and political identities, but who have to co-exist in their diverse characteristics. This chapter argues that *Mūgithi*, as music and performative act, becomes crucial in integrating the disparate lifestyles in the city in the day-to-day living. The form of performance and music, though often in the Gīkūyū language, accommodates almost every participant, or patron in the bar. But as argued before, music, as sound, has this talismanic tendency to bridge all gaps, as the universal language of humankind. Waterman (1990: 213) elucidates the point while discussing *Jùjú* music of Nigeria:

> ... the most important link between ... performance practice and the distribution of power is the role of music as a metaphor of social order. Juju performance evokes a coherent multisensory image of a communal society, thoroughly cosmopolitan, yet firmly rooted in deep Yoruba values and sentiments.

Similar sentiments can be attributed to *Mūgithi*. It is only in a *Mūgithi* club where all reticence is disregarded as patrons, unknown to each other, celebrate the climax of the performance by linking up in a dance movement, hereinafter referred to as *Mūgithi* (train) which will involve everyone on the dance floor, irrespective of their disparate backgrounds. In this sense, the cosmopolitan nature of the performances comes out clear.

The two terms, one-man guitar and *Mūgithi* are quite interchangeable. One-man guitar refers to a singer-guitarist backed up, at most, by just a drummer. *Mūgithi* is "train" in the Gīkūyū language. In the performance, there are no defined steps, and the participants, (mostly patrons in a bar) are linked by holding on to the waist or shoulders of the one ahead. Though the actual *Mūgithi* may take up only a few minutes of an entire night of undiluted revelry, it has come to define the night and has almost become an anthem[9] in most clubs around Nairobi.

Coplan's (1982:124) assertion on the urbanisation of African music and development of distinct urban music styles, becomes powerful in this regard:

> Styles emerge out of the set of economic, political, social and cultural relations between musicians and the total context in which they perform. Such relationships depend upon channels of communication, the distribution of power in the environment, economic and other rewards from various performance alternatives, the demands of the sponsors and other participants, available stylistic resources, processes of performance training and competition and cooperation among performers.

Though the whole set of conditions may not apply for the origin of *Mūgithi*, most of them can as will be seen below. *Mūgithi* performance has introduced a new mode of music, where musicians have had to deal with limited resources. At the same time, the new style, which is enjoying popularity amidst an outburst of digitalized music, signifies a major shift in the music and entertainment circles in Kenya. The artistes' indulgence in taboo subjects like sex, which earlier artists hardly touched on, points to a major innovation in Kenyan music. However, hedonistic as the *Mūgithi* craze may seem, it was, ironically, adopted from those familiar all-night religious *keshas* (charismatic prayer vigils) where the Christians link up to "join the train to heaven" with Jesus as the driver of the train.

The one-man guitar craze can be traced to the late 1990s. Amidst the economic depression characteristic of this period in Kenya, many club owners resorted to hiring solo artists, instead of entire bands, which would mean higher costs. The effect of economic depression did not only apply to the club but to the artists as well who had to make do with rudimentary and less expensive instruments. It was also a kind of cultural return to the music of the 1960s and 1970s, which afforded the interaction between the artists and patrons.[10] Again, unlike in the past when traditional music was embraced by people with a strong rural background, as Kariuki

(1998) argues, 'a growing number of urban based musicians are turning to music they either heard during music festivals or from their parents'.[11]

The late Jean Bosco Mwenda[12] is credited with having started it all. Armed only with his guitar – no back-up drummer, as is the trend now – Mwenda was well known for his cover versions of western pop classics. At Ngong Hills Hotel, he found particular demand for cover versions of popular Gĩkũyũ and Swahili numbers, which he often flavoured with his own lyrics.

The origin of the *Mũgithi* performance can also be linked to what Ndigirigi accounts for the proliferation 'bar productions'. Faced with low audience turnout in conventional theatre halls, performers 'literally followed the audience where they frequent most' (1999: 90). Musicians have followed suit and have redefined the bar in urban centers as a space for performance. A criticism leveled against the bar productions is that they deal with issues of sexuality *ad nauseam*. Ndigirigi (1999: 90) argues that the quality of such productions is generally poor:

> The audience (which drinks beer during the performances with waiters moving in between the seats to take orders) is normally looking for entertaining diversion and not a quality performance. The bawdier the performances, the merrier the audiences.

However, this is not necessarily the case. Quality theatre productions and music productions as well, have emanated from this tradition. Successful musicians like Them Mushrooms, Bilenge Musica amongst others continue to attract huge crowds at Simmers Restaurant in Nairobi's central business district.

The bar here may be seen in the same light with the *shebeen* in South Africa which provided a place for the interaction 'necessary for urban African social survival and the musical blending of cultural influences and produced many innovative and distinctive urban South African urban performance styles' (Coplan, 115). In fact, *marabi*[13], a whole new musical style in South Africa was born there as Minky Schlesinger (1993:14) argues. In relation to the above, the argument here is that *Mũgithi* performance has curved a niche in most urban restaurants and beer halls. The proliferation of *Mũgithi* artists even outside Nairobi, attests to this.

On typical busy nights (Fridays and Saturdays)[14], action begins at around 8pm, when musicians start by giving patrons slow numbers ranging from English to Kiswahili oldies. This is the time of the night when most people are just settling down and it is a challenge to begin gradually working them up. By 11pm, the pattern is switched to playing up-tempo cover versions of more contemporary hits.

In fact most one-man guitarists follow a systematic order on any night. They start mostly with renditions of songs by popular country musicians like Kenny Rogers, then to gospel hymns. As the night wears on, they introduce local songs by renowned Kenyan musicians. Towards midnight, they bring in the funky beat, by redoing songs popular with the youth. The switch to traditional music finally opens the floor to the *Mūgithi* performance. Seen in almost the same light as traditional music like Mwomboko, *Mūgithi* dwells on redoing almost all songs, even the ones without sexually explicit tones, by corrupting the lyrics. Traditional music used heavily allusive language when engaging on themes of sex and sexuality. However, for the artiste to accommodate the disparate classes of people, a rendition of the traditional music as well as the contemporary becomes crucial.

The real *Mūgithi* action begins after midnight, when most patrons are on their feet and, properly intoxicated, free of all inhibitions. This is when the "adults only" segment begins. Mike Murimi, one of the artists says, "I realised that blending new wording and beats to the song, rather than simply singing straight, was more appealing to the audience," (Ngaira, 2002) He adds that it is due to the pressure from revellers that he uses the trademark bawdy lyrics, but he is quick to point out that naughty songs are not the main ingredient of his shows or the reason for his success.

In the one-man-guitar and the *Mūgithi* performance, there's the copying and parodying of music done by renowned artists, reworking or reproducing famous originals, releasing self-sufficient tunes into the flux of the dance hall. These reproductions are the products of experiential ownership and this experience then stimulates variants and even new work. Like Middleton (1990: 96) asserts:

> Analogous processes operate for listeners too. Music users (listeners, patrons, dancers) often sing along, identifying with the vocal, appropriating the song, making the performance their own; forgotten or indecipherable lyrics may be replaced by substitutes-anything as

long as the rhythmic-melodic articulation is maintained. The result
is more interesting than the original.

The practices of appropriation, therefore, are glimpses of the possibility of a new form of composition inscribed within a new cultural ecology, which might ultimately supersede the category of art. It would be in Enzensberger's words (1976: 36-7) 'an aesthetic which is not limited to the sphere of the artistic'.

However, the term 'appropriate' may be inappropriate in this discussion. This is so because what one might refer to as really authentic music is appropriated music. As Connell and Gibson (2003: 108) argue, 'while musical histories tend to identify 'authentic' origins and examples of regional uniqueness, music scenes have almost always been replicated across vast distances'. Popular music in the view espoused in this research thus remains transient, emerging and dissipating as fashions change and generations pass. It is integrated into what Middleton (1990: 138) calls, 'subjectively motivated' social practice. If constitution and reconstitution of meaning is occurring in the lyrics, this practice may be thought of as 'subjectively motivated', where such practice is 'orientated around the existence of a social group; however ephemeral, partial or geographically diffuse, all essentials of popular music are present in a generalized form' (ibid).

Musical objects, however integrated into particular social practices, always carry the marks of their (contradictory) origins and of other (real or potential) existences. This then raises the question of how they relate to particular social locations.

In a *Mūgithi* night, patrons experience renditions of song done by established popular musicians, for instance, the guru of Gīkūyū music Joseph Kamaru, Kakai Kilonzo, the renowned maestro of Eastern Kenya *benga*[15], Musaimo, Queen Jane, amongst others. This is brought about by the need to accommodate the disparate age groups, which patronize most of these restaurants and bars. Once in a while, the artist will introduce renditions of songs by musicians from all over the world, but subtly done in the local vernacular, but somehow retains the beat and the rhythm. As argued above, this is a conscious effort, or financial strategy to give the performance a national and remotely global outlook.[16]

Of the most popular rendition, among most one-man guitarists (Salim Junior, Mike Rua and Mike Murimi) is Tabu Ley's hit *Muzina*. Tabu Ley is a famous musician from former Zaire, and whose music is still very popular amongst Kenyans. The Gĩkũyũ have a male name, almost similar to this, Micina. The Jamaican ragga duo Chaka Demus and Pliers' song, *Murder She Wrote* is also quite popular, and corrupted as *Mama Cirũ*, literally meaning the Mother of Cirũ (a short form of Wanjirũ). A Luhya wedding song, (*Ng'ombe*), Princess Julie's *Dunia Mbaya*, Kalenjin Sisters' song, *Magtalena*, are all re-done in the Gĩkũyũ language thus forging a synthesis of the best of local traditional cultures and foreign modern life ways and technologies. Several examples suffice.

The *Mũgithi* performance, having originated from the prayer night-vigils, as indicated above, incorporates popular gospel songs. Most of them though are corrupted to fit the secular mood of the performance. One song, *Kuma Ndaiga Mĩrigo Thĩ* (Since I Let go my Burdens) in Christian discourses is meant to express the joy of the singer, after leaving the sinful life. It is a song full of praise for the Lord. But Mike Murimi, one of the leading one man guitarists, gives it explicit connotations, for a girl, who 'letting go her burdens', means acceding to a young man's sexual pursuits. *Mĩrigo* may mean burdens, but in popular discourse, especially among the youth, means the genitalia!

The corruption of the popular gospel songs might be indicative of a feeling of inadequacy in Christianity, an exotic spirituality, which is best expressed by a number of traditional Gĩkũyũ songs in a *Mũgithi* night[17]. Traditional forms such as *Mwomboko*[18] are ubiquitous in any performance, and again a pointer to the different age entities in the audience. But it could also be indicative of how song travels and acquires new meaning in different contexts. The songs retain most of the gospel lyrics, but with snippets of vulgar language filtering throughout the songs. For instance, the original version of "*Mĩrigo Thĩ*" (Gĩkũyũ: Since I Let go my Burdens) goes.

> *Kairĩtu gaka* - young girl
> *Ũiguaga atĩa* - how does it feel?
> *Kuma waiga mĩrigo thĩ* - after you let go your burdens.

The response:

> *Njiguaga o kũgoca* – I just feel like praising God
> *Kuma ndaiga mĩrigo thĩ* - Since I let go my burdens.

Then follows the corrupt version. And the girl's response is distorted:

> *Njiguaga o kũgoca* – I feel like like praising
> *Ma ya Ngai nĩĩ* – I swear by God
> *Tiga kuma hĩndĩ ĩrĩa ndahoirwo*- when he made sexual advances to me
> *Nĩĩ ngĩona ndingĩkira rĩngĩ* – I decided never to remain silent
> *Nokĩo njiguaga o kũgoca* – that's why I always feel like praising
> *Kuma ndaiga mĩrigo thĩ* – since I let go my burdens

The *Mũgithi* artiste here appears to give a gospel song such lewd connotations, which leaves the audience craving for more. The huge success of *Mũgithi* as exhibited in the song arises from the interplay between the secular and religious. Harping on the popularity of the gospel song, the artistes then introduces the sex theme, which is never a topic in religious circles, and manages to negotiate the blur boundaries between the mundane and the spiritual.

Mũgithi, like Bakhtinian's carnivalesque (1968:15) involves the 'temporary suspension of all hierarchic distinctions and barriers among men ... and of the prohibitions of usual life'. During the performance, the normal constraints and conventions of the everyday world are thrown off.

In the Bakhtinian carnivalesque, parody, satire and insult directed at the authorities were couched in the festivities where there was enlarging, exuberant laughter at the arbitrariness that lock people in their spaces. Similarly, in *Mũgithi*, there is the liberating humour, but which is more inward-looking. The artists as well as the audience, especially during the call-response moment laugh at themselves, mock themselves. These songs at the same time are also reflective on the social realities in Kenya, the social change occasioned by urbanization, but most important in Mũgithi is the play on rural and urban identities, realized through language.

But with the suspension of hierarchy in this performance, the reveler from the village will be as comfortable as his or her colleague from the city as they inhabit the same social space, the utopian ideal of an egalitarian society, yet in everyday living, this is not the case. In the same way, this can be read as a social critique to the postcolonial authority that has neglected development in rural areas and concentrated all its efforts to appease the middle class, the class of the ruling elite!

It is against this background coupled with the fact that the performance is mostly an urban phenomenon[19] that I strive to bring out *Mūgithi* performance as a site where urban identities are performed. While talking about identities, Stokes' (1994:114) evinces:

> Musicians ... today experience place and identity in ways, which embrace many of the characteristic contradictions and ambiguities of modernity and its legacy. More often than not they are separated from their cultural locus by a gulf of time and space: the discourses in which place is constructed and celebrated in relation to music have never before had to permit such flexibility and ingenuity.

While discussing urban identities in the one-man guitar and *Mūgithi* phenomenon, it is the ambiguities and contradictions of modernity that this chapter engages with. Being an emergent trend in the Kenyan music scene, a parallel study with musicians of yore is quite important, but should not cloud its distinct features. Contrasting the urban space *vis-à-vis* the village thus becomes a defining moment while taking a look at urban identities in the said music. Urban identities are discussed from various angles namely, the space where the performance takes place, thematic concerns and the language used.

The one-man guitar and the resultant *Mūgithi* performance is mostly rooted in the life of the urban population, where artists exploit the interest of the urban masses in crime, corruption, adventure and intrigue, sex, love, romance, conflicts of cultures, linguistic innovations, idiosyncrasies and stereotypes. As Okwonkwo (1986:651) notes, when people are introduced to city life with its 'novelty and exacting demands' there's intensification of the search for new habits and new values.

The music of the one-man guitar is firmly rooted in contemporary urban society and reflects the 'interests and conflicts of its transitional nature as a meeting point between new western values and old traditional concepts' (Okwonkwo, 1986: 653). Most incidents in the music are taken from the everyday urban life, and they are able to capture both the restless excitement, the frustrations of life in the city and its ramifications.

The fact that the *Mūgithi* performance takes place mostly in urban bars and clubs points to a dialectic relation between music and space. The argument here is that music shapes spaces and spaces shape music. In various ways, as Connell and Gibson (2003:192) assert, sounds have been used 'to create spaces and simulate patterns of human behaviour in particular locations'. The kind of discourse *Mūgithi* and one-man artists engage in their song and performance will look completely out of space if performed, say, in a stadium or in an open-air market stage. No wonder, this is music hardly aired on most radio stations in Kenya.

Several striking signifiers define the space of *Mūgithi* performance. Given that this mostly happens in bars and restaurants, beer drinking is inevitable. There is a shared community of patrons that frequent the bar. Some kind of carnival atmosphere is created within the *Mūgithi* space in which certain realities are suspended and new ones introduced. The performance creates and celebrates its own world and its own set of moralities.

The carnival nature of *Mūgithi* offers the participants a cathartic effect to experience a world out of the normal lived reality. Notes Bakhtin (1968: 34):

> The carnival spirit offers the chance to have a new outlook on the world, to realize the relative nature of all that exists and to enter a completely new order of things.

There is a motivation during this carnival time during *Mūgithi* to create a form of human social configuration that lies beyond existing social forms. For a nation that is so divided along ethnic lines, especially politically, during the performance, as seen above, a sense of egalitarianism exists, where people from different classes, communities and religions fuse into one apparent homogenous entity.

But again, the parallel association of music and performance in a bar, with 'social license, sexual adventure and drinks, establishes the performance as a vital and pleasurable part of life' (Stokes, 12-3). In the same vein, the performance in the bar is used to create a sense of space as well as to 'reaffirm various social identities and challenges in which everyday, urban spaces are gendered in particular ways' (Connell and Gibson, 2003: 193).

The performance and reception of *Mūgithi,* therefore, in particular locations, in this case the bar, may provide an 'effective form of resistance to the homogenizing forces of the culture industry' (Smith, 1994:237), not necessarily by producing an alternative sound, since most of these songs are renditions, but by enabling people to experience music in distinctive localized ways, to suit their demands. This in turn provides a means through which a sense of 'urbanity' is created and contested, especially when you consider the thematic concerns of most of these songs.

The one-man guitarists who entertain revellers in nightclubs in big cities, like Nairobi specialize on renditions of popular songs but they infuse them with subverted lyrics. The theme of sex becomes quite prominent amongst many. The prominence of the sex theme accentuates the idea that cultural and social norms are not strictly adhered to in urban settings unlike in the villages. The fact that the one-man guitarists only perform in nightclubs in major towns confirms this fact. The guitarists therefore redefine and create a new audience and space for their music. The urban setting being cosmopolitan in nature encompasses people from all cultures and settings.

Sex, infidelity, prostitution are the most overt themes and the explicit lyrics, performed especially during the 'adults only' segment attest to this. This explains partly why the music is never aired in any broadcasting station in Kenya. In fact, smaller bars and hotels (unlike the bigger and renowned hotels which *pretend* to be offering family entertainment) deal with issues of sexuality in explicit terms.

In a corruption of Simon Kihara's (better known as Musaimo) *Cai wa 14,* one-man guitarist, Mike Rua assumes the *Ngūcū* beat, but subverts the lyrics to sexually explicit overtones:

> *Ndathiīte gūcera Majengo* – I went to Majengo[20] for a visit
> *Ngīnyua ūcūrū na kukumanga* – and drank porridge and aphrodisiac
> *Ngīgwata maraya ngīnina* – I slept with all prostitutes
> *Ngīambīrīria kūgwata ng'ombe* –till I started mounting cows

In *Mūgithi* performance, messages about the relativity and arbitrariness of the social conventions are experienced. The above lyrics can never be found in a normal conversation, especially where people from different age groups are gathered, but this is more like the norm in a *Mūgithi* night. The music concerns itself with 'the lower stratum of the body, the life of the belly, and the reproductive organs; it therefore relates to acts of defecation and copulation, conception, pregnancy and birth' (Bakhtin, 1968: 21). What can be gleaned from the above is that the melodramatic representation of sex and sexuality is actually meant to evoke laughter and merriment as well as some relief, since sex and related subjects in Kenya are shrouded in some mystery and the subject hardly appears in public discourses.

In most Kenyan communities, sex is not usually discussed openly, unlike the pre-colonial days when people received sex education through the performance of puberty rites. Due to urbanization and industrialization, these rites are seldom performed. When a proposal to include family life education in Kenyan schools was put forward some years back, it was met with a lot of resistance. In 1996, the Catholic Church in Kenya participated in the burning of condoms, and other HIV/AIDS materials, as a protest towards the idea of introducing sex education in schools, a clear pointer to the conservative nature of most Kenyans[21]. But *Mūgithi* works to open up discourses on sex and sexuality by introducing them into the public domain

One-man guitarists have however transcended the sex and secrecy, and in their songs, sex, copulation, and overt mention of the genitalia form the mainstay of their performances. A clear example is the corruption of Sam Muraya's song, *Mama Kiwinya*, where artists Mike Murimi and Salim Junior engage in clear and explicit obscene language, but which fires up the audience. Mention of the genitalia, goes on *ad naseum*.

Ngahutia nyondo – I touch her breasts
Ngahutia kīnena – I touch her crotch
Ngahutia matina –I touch her behind
Ngahutia rūng'ūthū – I touch her private parts
Ngarīra– and I cry.

Departing from the earlier musicians with their over-used theme of romance and relationships, the one-man guitarist, opts not to present sex, copulation and the genitalia in a 'private, egoistic form, severed from the other spheres of life, but as something universal, representing all the people' (Bakhtin, 1968:19). In the Bakhtinian (ibid) sense of the grotesque realism:

> [a]bundance and the all people's element ... determine the gay and festive character of all images of bodily life; they do not reflect the drabness of everyday existence. The material bodily principle is a triumphant festive principle; it is a "banquet for all the world".

The climax of the evening is the *Mūgithi* performance where patrons join together in a 'train' dancing around the pub. The musicians in their lyrics call upon the participants to feel free to *'touch what you don't have'*. This is a sexual implication for members of the opposite sex in the audience to engage in all manners of sexual/romantic gestures while still on the floor. While people are holding each other's waist, there is the license in the performance for men and women to touch each other in a sexually suggestive manner. It is almost similar to the *patapata*[22] in a South African context. This sexual play in dance was so dominant a performance in most traditional and folk music amongst most Kenyan communities.

The interface between tradition and modernity is manifest in such regards. Though mostly an urban performance, tradition comes to haunt the *Mūgithi* space. By engaging in themes like sex, which are usually not in the public domain, the musicians are simply 'distracting us from reality, or substituting trivial concerns and encouraging decadent ideals and activities, values that are programmed in all of us in the consumer society', Jameson (1976: 14). Such works of art are ways of distorting and repressing reality. He continues:

> They do not speak about something essentially different from the content and material of revolutionary art; rather, the same fears and concerns ... only what they attempt to do is not to express, but rather to manage those fears ...

That sex and sexuality are inevitable topics in day to day life, the *Mūgithi* artists brings them in the public domain, to make the themes items of discussion especially in the era of HIV/AIDS which continues to afflict most third world countries. The silence on sex especially makes it difficult to educate the public on matters related to the syndrome.

As argued above, *Mũgithi* is mostly an urban performance. Themes of rurality or the country, as Ferguson (1992:80) argues, have often provided metaphors for the construction of indigenous critiques of urban, capitalist encroachment. The village is associated with moral purity as contrasted to the town, which is conceived as 'immoral, artificial, corrupt and anomic' (ibid). One-man guitarists deviate from this conventionality. Unlike most local popular musicians in Kenya, one-man-guitarists are overtly concerned with the celebration of the city and its perceived ills while mocking the village. The city is not seen as a 'sea, which has drowned many', as musician Joseph Kariuki in the previous chapter describes Nairobi. It is seen as an opportune space for one to earn a livelihood. It offers a glimmer of hope towards economic emancipation. Musicians like Joseph Kamaru and D.K. Kamau in the earlier days always castigated the city and its entrapments, singling out prostitution and the good-time girls who would fleece working and married men all their wages and salaries. The village has been celebrated as virtuous while the city is evil, but *Mũgithi* artists work to subvert this paradigm in celebration of modernity as signified in the city.

In most of these songs by earlier musicians, men drawn into dissipating pleasures of urban women and the fast life are castigated. In a song by Joseph Kamaru, a man tells of his long journey to come and see his darling in town. Having not seen her for some time, he is taken aback when he discovers another man's outfit in her wardrobe. To cushion this shock, he rushes to the shops for breakfast, but on returning, he finds used condoms in the room, and his hunger disappears.

But the one-man guitar seems to pick from here. In echoing themes of the village and the city, most lyrics in these songs portray the rural folk as a backward and primitive society where notions of romance are foreign to them. A song tells of this man from the village that meets a girl in town. A kiss from the girl leaves the man dazzled that he nearly faints! So, for participants to convince others during a *Mũgithi* night that they are not from the village, they engage in the weirdest sexual gestures on the floor. These musicians do not apportion blame to prostitutes and sweet-time girls, but lash out at the 'primitive' man from the village who cannot cope with the fast life in the city.

Sex and drinking, which previously marked the city as evil, become positive icons of modernity and the freedom of space and body that comes with the city in *Mūgithi* performance. What seems to have been treated as evil by the ambiguous and double discourse of modernity (for example the Christian influence and its tendency to cast away reference to sex as evil) is reversed. There are certain subtleties that connect *Mūgithi* with Mwomboko, a traditional Gĩkũyũ genre in which there were no inhibitions on matters of sex and sexuality.

The ambiguity expressed in *Mūgithi* can be traced in this interface between *Mūgithi* and *Mwomboko*, or rather modernity and tradition. Notes Masolo (2000: 377):

> ... due to socio-geographical concentration, the new musical tastes and styles [are] associated with the loose lures of urbanism. Even as the new guitar styles become popularly embraced, the conservative voice of tradition continues to regard them with moral contempt and suspicion. Widely associated with the moral permissiveness or decadence of the cities, the "modern" was in some ways seen as "corrupt" and "immoral" at the same time as it was admired as a "good" and "desirable" sign of new elitism.

The above at best describes the moral ambiguity of the modern music, especially *Mūgithi,* which enables the performance to draw audiences from all spheres of life.

The irony of the whole *Mūgithi* performance is that despite lambasting the village, which is supposed to be unspoilt by western values, the artistes use vernacular in almost all songs; in this case, Gĩkũyũ. However, the suggestion here is not that the village is the custodian of vernacular languages. But given the cosmopolitan setting of the city, several vernaculars fuse into slang in Nairobi, called *sheng*[23]. It is therefore feasible to say that most vernacular speakers are mostly found in villages, where levels of inter-tribal interactions are minimal. However, this research acknowledges the fact that the migratory nature of the labour force, from the city to the village transports a number of urban styles, of dress, language and music. The argument here is that *Mūgithi* occupies a liminal space, bearing the past as it embraces the present. Traditional songs, like *Mwomboko, Ngũcũ*, where cultural values are exalted, play a major role in a *Mūgithi* night, but enjoyed and danced to by the diverse groups that patronize *Mūgithi* joints. The village, thus, is cast both as backward in some ways, but also as a bearer of wisdom and morality.

Much however can be said of the duplicitous nature of the 'country'[24] much as it can be said of the 'city'. Thus, as Haugerud (1995:139) asserts, presumed boundaries between town and countryside, like those between town and countryside are fuzzy at best.

Mūgithi performance, succeeds in bringing disparate identities together. For a first-timer to a *Mūgithi* night, the form of entertainment is alluring, but so is the variety of patrons. It has become a space where anybody – no boundary of class or status – will mingle freely and let their hair down with wild abandon; where the *matatu* tout will mingle freely with the high-powered corporate executive. This is where all inhibitions are cast aside as Ngaira (2002), notes:

> Total strangers mark the climactic moment by linking up in a *Mūgithi*, which will snake across the dance floor, negotiate its way around tables and every available place. Everybody – the matronly housewife, the quiet academic, the shy, church-going girl, the noisy politician, the garrulous *matatu* driver, the repressed accountant and the lady of easy virtue – will joyously sing together, as one, the bawdiest lyrics imaginable.

The end result is the blurring of perceived disparities – urban/rural, men/women, employed/unemployed, student/teacher etc. Popular music, in this case, *Mūgithi* reflects the fluxes and fluidity of contemporary life, unsettling binary oppositions established in earlier phases of modernity (tradition/contemporary, authentic/inauthentic, local/global), thus enhancing the dynamic nature of music.

Conclusion

Mūgithi demonstrates the audiences' willingness to mingle freely despite the diverse backgrounds, as they assert their diversity. Musical style, as this chapter argues may articulate and define communal values in heterogeneous, rapidly transforming societies. The very act of naming a genre, in this case, *Mūgithi*, as Kiel (1985:126), suggests, may be a declaration of cultural consolidation. This augments Anderson's (1983:15) notion of the imagined communities, who asserts that 'all communities larger than the primordial villages of face-to-face (and perhaps even these) are imagined. Communities are to be distinguished, not by their falsity/genuineness, but by the style in which they are imagined'. Musical metaphor thus plays a role in the imaginative modeling of the Kenyan urban society as a hierarchy in communal values, comprised of interdependent, yet unequal actors. *Mũgithi* performance style portrays an imagined community of a large number of people, 'a solidarity that no one individual could know through first-hand experience – and embodies the ideal affective texture of social life and the melding of new and old, exotic and indigenous, within a unifying syncretic framework' (Waterman, 1990:221)

However, this chapter concludes by arguing that urban identities are not fixed identities. They are not created inside a self-contained urban grouping but at a site of many overlapping identities/players including the villager, the 'urbanite', the foreigner, etc. It is, thus, difficult to talk of pure urban identities and the *Mũgithi* performance best attests to this. The recreation of rural identities through language, dance and the performance (again these identities are not fixed, and exhibit ambiguities) in music and dance by the urban folks, point to the complex relationship of ethnicities and class identities another broad area tackled in the next chapter. The deliberate choice of language clearly emphasizes its cultural and political significance. As Connell and Gibson (2003: 134) argue, 'music and language remain potent and ubiquitous markers of ethnic identity'.

Notes

[1] The word '*Mũgithi*' is derived from '*mixsi*' a term used in the 1950s to refer to a particular train that ferried both passengers and cargo in the same compartments. Probably the earlier version of third class, and maybe the only train Africans could ride, then. The etymology of *Mũgithi* is "Mixed train" which Nairobi youth in the 1950s referred to as simply "*mixsi*". A Gĩkũyũ rendition of "Mixsi" would assume linguistic features common in other word borrowings. For instance, "s" is realized as "th" (e.g. *thogithi,* for socks, *thothenji* for sausage), "mi-" for noun class marker. I acknowledge *Mzee* Jeremiah Mũtonya's oral explanation of the term *Mũgithi* and Mũngai Mũtonya for the linguistic analysis. All translations of song excerpts from the Gĩkũyũ language are done by the author himself.

[2] Aware of the diverse interpretations of this tradition/modernity dyad, especially in postcolonial studies, this chapter appropriates a geographical angle to delineate the urban/

rural divide as expressed in the performance of *Mūgithi*. As Brodnicka (2003: 2) is wont to remind us, it is always important to 'differentiate the ideology of tradition and modernity from tradition or modernity as they are experienced'.

[3] Shebeens are taverns in black populated townships in South Africa, which have continually provided space for cultural expressions among the young blacks.

[4] It is this interaction, as David Coplan (1982: 115) argues, that gives rise to innovative and creative urban perform styles.

[5] *Nyatiti* is an 8-stringed plucked lyre from the Luo community located in western Kenya. *Litungu* is also a lyre, mostly seven-stringed, a traditional instrument from the Luhya community in Western Kenya too. However, the Gīkūyū too had a one-string instrument, *wandīndī*. The influence of these traditional instruments has defined the various emergent guitar styles emerging in Kenya.

[6] *Benga* was born when Luo dance rhythms were pushed into the acoustic guitar. *Benga* in fact is a Luo word meaning 'soft and beautiful'.

[7] Doug Paterson and John Low characterize this as the finger-style, which was played on dry guitars.

[8] With the development of this music, lady musicians have entered the fray and are referred to as one-lady guitar. Their songs are devoid of the bawdy lyrics that characterise performances of their male counterparts, but the form and nature of the performance remains the same. Florence Wangari wa Kabera is the pioneer of this female tradition.

[9] Anthems are normally the undisputed positions of the musical presentation of place. Played in almost all the night clubs, dance halls and bars in most urban Kenyan centers, *Mūgithi* has ascertained its position as most clubs' favourite.

[10] See Masolo's article on the Nyatiti among the Luo community in Kenya.

[11] John Kariuki (1998), in trying to explain why Kenyan musicians presently are looking back for lyrical inspiration insists 'in a business where timing is everything, the burn-out of Congolese music largely due to over-exposure and self-parody, as well as lack of interesting new music from the rest of the world, may be the deciding factor. And to many artistes, going back to the roots is the logical course of action'. *Daily Nation,* September 6, 1998.

[12] Jean Mwenda's acoustic–guitar style was quite popular in Kenya in the late forties and fifties. His style, combined with the rhythms and vocals from *bodi*, a ceremonial music sung by Luo women has been considered as the origin of *Benga*, a distinctive Kenyan

music style (see Stapleton and May, 1989:233). Interesting to note that the one-man guitar phenomenon is also credited to Mwenda's guitar style.

[13] See Denis-Constant Martin in Reebee Garofalo's (ed), *Rocking the Boat* (1992:197) where he avers that '*marabi*, South African jazz and even *kwela* were the offspring of a mixture: music from the city, in which supposedly tribal origins disappeared to make way for the input of all'.

[14] Kenyans refer to Friday as "*members' day*, which significantly marks the beginning of the weekend. The Friday evening culture involves all the extracurricular activities especially for most working people and 'clubbing' (dancing and drinking) is the major activity.

[15] *Benga* was born when Luo dance rhythms were pushed into the acoustic guitar. *Benga* in fact is a Luo word meaning 'soft and beautiful'. But with time, other variations of *benga* emerged, as explained in the introductory chapter. Kilonzo's variation is what I am referring to as Eastern Kenya *benga*.

[16] Until recently, none of the music has been properly recorded, thus cannot go beyond the walls of the restaurant. The recording, of live performances produces tapes of quite poor quality, but which sell widely due to the popularity of *Mūgithi*.

[17] However, this can be subjected to a number of other possibilities.

[18] *Mwomboko* was a traditional Gīkūyū dance of young people where a couple moved two steps forward, stooped and made a turn. Men pressed their partners to their chests, and occasionally spun them around

[19] *Mūgithi* can be said to have started in Nairobi. It is only recently that the performance has spread its tentacles to Mombasa, and it is fast spreading to other smaller towns in Kenya, like Nakuru and Thika.

[20] Majengo is a famous Nairobi slum, known for the commercial sex industry.

[21] See Lynne Muthoni Wanyeki, 'Kenya-Population: Church Burns Condoms and AIDS Materials' *InterPress News Service (IPS); 5 September 1996. Again, in 2003, a parents' caucus in Kenya fronted a crusade to ban Chinua Achebe's book, A Man of the People and other two textbooks from the secondary school syllabus.* Those pushing for the ban on the books picked excerpts from *A Man of the People*, which they said were clearly explicit and were likely to excite the students' imagination and stir their sexual desires. See Mwangi (2003) Such instances denote clearly the conservative nature of Kenyans, especially in matters related to sex and sexuality, which however, have been subverted by *Mūgithi* artists.

[22] Also *phata-phata*, *pathapatha* in Xhosa and Zulu. *Phatha* is touch, feel, thus touch-touch. It is a sexually suggestive dance-style in which pairs of dancers touch each other's bodies with their hands, a dance tempo popularized by Miriam Makeba.

[23] Sheng has been defined as an acronym for Swahili-English slang, developed in Nairobi in post-independence Kenya. This innovation however incorporates also lexical items, not just from the two national /official languages, but also from the wide array of the linguistic diversity defines the Kenyan nation. For more on Sheng, see Githiora, Chege (2002), Githinji, Peter (2006) and Mutonya, Mungai (2007).

[24] Ferguson, (1992:90) asserts that the imagined locus of moral purity and wholeness of the village, as contrasted to the city, obscures the reality of the village too as the 'seat of actual and antagonistic social relations'.

CHAPTER SIX

Mũgithi Performance: Popular Music, Stereotypes and Ethnic Identity

Mũgithi performance, mostly an urban phenomenon in Kenya can best be described as a 'heterophonous order of segmentary identities creating a resonant ensemble whose constituent self and group allegiances become experientially fused in musical celebration'[1] Parkes, (1994:158). The composite and cosmopolitan nature of the urban settings, and subsequently the *Mũgithi* performance together with its carnival nature comes close to Parkes' experience in Pakistan. The mixture of the patrons from all walks of life makes the fusion of different identities easier in the *Mũgithi* performances. It is one instance where music brings the people together. Significantly though, this music is mostly performed and sang in the Gĩkũyũ language, despite the ethnic plurality in Kenya. Ethnic stereotypes and parodies are constant themes in the lyrics. The chapter problematises the contradictory complexities and ambiguities of the postcolony; is *Mũgithi* a Gĩkũyũ performance or does its heterogeneous audience make it a national project? Is the *Mũgithi* performance a means of expressing Gĩkũyũ nationalism, a way of Gĩkũyũ cultural revival/renaissance or does its multi-ethnic following points towards the role of music as a response to unfavourable political conditions? The chapter also analyses the political factors, which explain the genesis of the music in the 1990s, as it grapples with the issues raised above.

Mũgithi ũyũ x3 –	This train
Mũgithi ũyũ wa Daytona[2] -	This trainof Daytona
Salim nĩwe ndereba, Mũgithi ũyũ x4 -	Salim is the train driver
Ũthiaga ũkĩgambaga -	The train makes
Chuchuchuchu -	The chuchuchu sound
Mũndũ ahutie kĩrĩa atarĩ -	Touch what you don't have[3],
Mũgithi ũyũ, x4 –	In this train

The above marks the climax of a *Mũgithi* night (mostly late in the night when the greater part of the audience has had one-too-many) where patrons in a bar or night club glide along in a snake or train-like formation. The dancers are linked by holding on to the waist or shoulders of the one ahead. The climax marks the end of a night, where the one-man guitar, a solo performer takes the audience through a whole range of lyrics, some original, but most of them appropriations and renditions of popular songs. Themes in the lyrics range from religion, romance, and sex, and most artists often use sexually explicit lyrics. Music from the artists comes in all languages, Lingala, Luo, Gĩkũyũ, Swahili, English, etc. The previous chapter has shown how this performance incorporates people from all walks of life irrespective of gender, age or ethnicity. This phenomenon is mostly prevalent in major urban centres in Kenya.

It is important to note that one-man guitar and *Mũgithi* are not synonymous. Over years, the idea of a solo performer entertaining an audience with music other than his or her own has been an integral part in what we might call the bar or the night club culture. The artists in this chapter become important in the sense that *Mũgithi* has to crown their performances.

> At the popular political level, music and dance have become an inseparable part of political visibility and dignitarism. In the guise of entertainment, it often serves as a form of social and political discourse, a performed statement of popular acceptance, enhancement and legitimation of socially and politically coveted statuses and roles. In these senses, music and dance become signifiers of social and political hierachizations. (Masolo, 2000:368)

In the run-up to the 2002 general elections in Kenya, popular music was an integral political campaign tool. The political temperatures at the time propelled songs to national fame. GidiGidi MajiMaji's song *Unbwogable* is a telling testimony, as Hofmeyr, Ogude and Nyairo (2003) have explicated in their article on popular culture in Kenya. *Mũgithi* is then understood in this light. When Mwai Kibaki, the presidential aspirant fronted by the coalition of opposition parties (known as the National Rainbow Coalition, NARC), was returning to Kenya after weeks of hospitalization in London in December 2002, the city was abuzz with all sorts of activities. Notes Rugene and Njeru (2002) in a newspaper article:

> Hundreds of "Kibaki for President" posters, stickers, badges, handbills caps and T-shirts were distributed to the supporters, some

of who wore outfits in Rainbow colours. As they awaited Mr Kibaki's arrival, the Narc supporters danced to the popular Gĩkũyũ *Mũgithi* and a corrupted version of GidiGidi MajiMaji's *Unbwogable[4]*.

Mention of *Mũgithi* here evokes a few issues. *Mũgithi* is an urban phenomenon is marked by cosmopolitanism, where age, race, tribe and gender identities are shelved as participants dance around the club or the dance hall. The allegory of the opposition unity in 2002 is played out in the *Mũgithi* performance as well as the above scenario, where people from all walks of life had come to welcome their key presidential candidate. Prior to this though, *Mũgithi* had continually played out diversity among the patrons especially in urban settings.

However, questions abound in the above analysis. Given that the presidential hopeful was from the Gĩkũyũ ethnic group, was this the reason why the crowds invoked this particular music? But didn't the crowd have a national outlook given that Kibaki was a candidate fronted by the various parties? What about the invoking of *Unbwogable*? The backbone of this chapter endeavors to understand the varying circumstances, political and social, which might have precipitated the vast growth of *Mũgithi* and answer questions to whose interests, this music serves.

Viewing music as a political-moral category[5] may help us understand the issues raised above. The last decade of Daniel arap Moi's regime (1990s) witnessed a serious crackdown and suppression of art forms, which were otherwise thought to be subversive. Editors were sent to jail, musicians were arrested and their music banned from the national broadcaster, plays were banned as well. The musician as a political activist has borne the brunt of government censor[6]. *Mũgithi* performance and the one-man guitar phenomenon proliferated in this shaky background. Music with an otherwise social and direct message would not escape the government censor's eyes. Few examples of Gĩkũyũ songs[7] suffice: David Karanja's song, *Gĩtumia Gĩkĩ* (This Other Woman) was a clear cry from a son who had been mistreated by the stepmother. The stepmother had caused much anguish in the family:

> *Baba ndũingate gĩtumia gĩkĩ* - Dad, please send this woman away
> *Nĩguo mũciĩ ũyũ witũ ũgĩe na thayũ* - So that we can have peace in our family

The authorities misinterpreted the song as a rebuke to the Moi government; that it was a prayer to God to send away Moi, from power, so that Kenya would be peaceful. The song was banned from the national broadcaster and records withdrawn from music shops. Peter Kigia's *Reke Tumanwo*, was also subjected to misinterpretation in the 1990s. The song is a lament of a marriage gone sour, and the protagonist is calling for an end to the affair. The song was given such serious political connotations.[8] Despite this censorship, *Mũgithi* still thrived. Whereas most of this music, which was banned, was properly recorded and submitted for airing, *Mũgithi* has existed mainly in bars and restaurants and this space has provided what its audience 'perceive as a world stage upon which the feelings of powerlessness could be expiated' (Stokes 1994:102). The informality of the performance helps it achieve the political goals.

As a response to the harsh political reality, this study views the *Mũgithi* performance as a form of passive resistance as James Scott is wont to tell us. In what Scott (1985:34) refers to as 'everyday resistance' as opposed to 'open defiance', *Mũgithi* comes out as the former, unlike the explicitly political lyrics in the run-up to the 1992 general elections in Kenya. Thus, *Mũgithi* has achieved much in conflating the discontent of the public, but in very subtle ways. Scott (1985:34) acknowledges that passive/everyday resistance is quite informal, often covert, and concerned largely with immediate *de facto* gains. He says;

> Open insubordination in almost any context will provoke a more rapid and ferocious response that an insubordination that may be as persuasive, but never ventures to contest the formal definitions of hierarchy and power.

The informality in the *Mũgithi* performance[9] explains how it gained prominence at the Coast after the infamous politically instigated tribal altercations between the indigenous coastal people and the upcountry folks in August 1997. The songs in the performance raised no eyebrows. The message in the lyrics then, while cosmopolitan in nature of revelry was also a chance to bravely hit back at the authorities for the political violence. It was very courageous considering the times but the main *Mũgithi* artists in Mombasa then came from Nairobi where the Moi era was in clear decline.[10] The courageous portrayal was crucial in changing the demeanor of the voters making them more brazen after having had a chance to thump the dictator.

The performance served as a rallying call for the *'watu wa bara'*[11] at the Coast to come together in the face of adversity. In the performance, it was not so much about what the musicians were singing about but about bringing together people from different backgrounds, who were under one imposing threat. *Mūgithi* then helped in the forging of 'temporary' identity, but in so doing laying an emphasis on the performance as a carnival where, as Morson and Emerson (1990:95) argue in tandem to Bakhtin's sense of the carnival that, 'individual responsibility disappears from view when the individual is merged into the great body of feasting people. There is no longer a self, there is only the carnival mask; ... Carnival as a whole appears to offer a perfect 'alibi for being''. Carnival, according to Bakhtin (1968:34) liberates by freeing us from all that is humdrum:

> This carnival spirit offers the chance to have a new outlook on the world, to realize the relative nature of all that exists and to enter a completely new order of things.

It is in bringing the disparate people[12] together, that the performance has articulated the sense and realization that in most circumstances, the resistance, or voicing of discontent can only succeed only to the extent that it hides behind the mask of public compliance, as Scott argues. The live performances in bars and restaurants became common occurrence, but behind it, the *Mūgithi* performance served a distinct political end especially when a group's existence was under threat.

Ideas about the special link between music and identity are frequently offered to explain why a particular social group – a community, a population, a nation – cultivates outmoded and seemingly irrelevant musical practice. In this case, ethnic identity is, therefore, invoked by individuals or social groups in particular circumstances, when it suits their purposes and helps them attain their goals.

Ngũgĩ wa Thiong'o, the renown Kenyan writer, in his novels has consistently used music as a means of both recognizing and reifying identity in the Kenyan situation. In novels such as *The River Between*, music is used to indicate polarities between groups with traditional Gĩkũyũ values and the Christian converts. In his other novel, *Petals of Blood*, contemporary popular culture is constructed partly through the discussion of musical and peri-musical phenomenon. *Devil on the Cross* looks at music as an agent for change within the postcolonial situation with Gatuiria, the music researcher developing a symphony drawing the various elements of Kenyan musical cultures together in an affirmation of an African national identity in the face of a rapacious colonial past.

Talking of ethnic identities, Barth, (1969:14) argues:

> Ethnic categories provide an organizational vessel that may be given varying amounts and forms of content in different socio-cultural systems. They may be of great relevance to behavior but they need not be; they may pervade all social life, or they may be relevant only in limited sectors of activity.

This approach by Barth, suggests then that music may be used in a more active manner. As Baily (1994:47) argues,

> 'music is itself a potent symbol of identity. Like language (and attributes of language such as accent and dialect), it is one of those aspects of culture, which can, when the need to assert 'ethnic identity' arises, most readily serve this purpose. Its effectiveness may be two-fold, as he continues; not only does it act as a ready means for the identification of different ethnic or social groups, but it has potent emotional connotations and can be used to negotiate identity in a particularly powerful manner'.

The rise of *Mūgithi* therefore in the late 1990s in Mombasa, and its use during the political campaigns of 2002 in Kenya can be explained in this way. The wide array of themes tackled in the music encompasses common problems afflicting the common person due to poor leadership.

In a rendition of Tabu Ley's *Muzina*, Mike Murimi, one of the leading *Mūgithi* artists, makes fun of a government policy, which was implemented in Kenya in 2001, when the national grid system was struggling to provide sufficient electricity to all citizens. A strategy of power rationing was thus introduced. Murimi sings of this man, whose wife gave birth at midnight, but they could not take her to hospital because the power had been rationed for that particular night!

Through the renditions and corruption of a number of popular songs across Kenya, Africa and the West, the music in the *Mũgithi* performance cuts across all barriers; ethnic, racial and gender, hence its wide appeal. The common identity one may identify here is one borne out of a confraternity in suffering. This chapter examines whether or not the popular appeal to a 'national audience' should be construed to mean that *Mũgithi* performance is a national endeavor.

Various songs in the *Mũgithi* performance are known to echo ethnic consciousness. On the ethno poetic stratagems in the lyrics and narration of the songs is the over-emphasis of stereotypes of the numerous ethnic categories in Kenya.[13] Certain subtleties restrict the songs purely to a Gĩkũyũ audience. This serves to portray the ambiguities and complexities of the *Mũgithi* performance. Even when the performance is largely an urban phenomenon, certain ethnic proclivities are manifest.

At the dawn of the 21st century, Kenya is ethnically divided more than ever before.[14] Ethnic chauvinism has particularly risen over the past 15 years mainly due to Moi's style of handling political challenges. The situation is more or less the same in most African countries, probably stemming from the nature of the ethnic diversity and the colonial legacy. Jewsiewicki and Buleli (2004:240) analyse the situation in subtle terms:

> The nation-state, while setting itself the task of merging ethnicities within the nation, institutionalises and perpetuates ethnicity. This ethnicity becomes a form of unfulfilled nationalism, a nationalism without a state, or even an initial element of the nation, necessary but insufficient in the absence of the state.

In Kenya, especially the 1990s, the situation was clearly manifested in the formation of the various opposition parties, especially after the advent of multi-party politics in 1991. The major political parties were seen as vehicles of the various communities to ascend to national leadership. The fragmented opposition in the 1992 enhanced the ruling party's under Daniel Moi, chances of winning the election, which they did. It is important to note from the above that ethnicity arose in opposition to the state, which Schatzberg (1988:22) argues is a consequence 'when a group feels excluded from the benefits the state has to offer and thus relatively disadvantaged'. However, while those in power find it prudent to manipulate ethnicity in ways that affect both themselves and the masses, the contradiction is normally manifest when 'national leaders regard any sub national identity, including ethnicity as a threat to nation-building and thus illegitimate' Schatzberg, (1988:25).

Politicians have worsened the situation by consciously mobilizing ethnic symbols and support to further their competition with others in the era of political pluralism. This is most evident in daily stereotypes and popular comedies, songs and newspaper cartoons, amongst other popular art forms.

Stereotypes are often over-generalized, negative and inaccurate. When they are negative, they lead us to expect negative behaviours from out groups. One of the reasons that stereotypes are retained is that they serve so many functions including helping people to maintain a positive self-image, justifying their social status and worldview. In the Kenyan context, especially in the previous two regimes, stereotypes have always existed and have been used to divide, instead of uniting people. The Gĩkũyũ and the Luo communities in the 1990s had always been seen as opposed to Moi's rule. In Moi's thoughts, he had clearly perceived the two communities in different lights:

> To Moi, the Gĩkũyũ are powerful because they are populous, industrious wealthy and self-reliant. But they are individualistic, greedy and selfish, thus vulnerable to goodies dangled before them at the right time. The Luo are populous too, but are easier to contain – one offhand and ill-considered remark about 'only 5000' being required to buy a Luo betrayed this attitude. But they are also troublemakers who love nothing better than a good riot, and in any case have no interest in national stability because they have no stake in the economy. They were also poisoned a long time ago with dangerous Marxist ideas.[15]

Moi had to latch onto these differences with a view of helping the two communities maintain the mistrust that has persisted since independence.

Odhiambo (2002:173) accentuates that the popular social models of 'the industrious Kikuyu and the lazy Luo were the results of colonial productions of knowledge; they have continued to inform the constant creation and recreation of ethnic categories in the postcolony'.

What's intriguing is that the *Mũgithi* musicians dwell so much on the perceived differences and stereotypes among other communities. One song, *Ukimwi Mbaya* by Mike Murimi suffices. A clear corruption of a popular AIDS awareness song by Princess Jully, the song calls for people to engage in safe sex by using condoms. The ridicule comes in the recommendations of how many condoms to use for different social/ethnic groups.

> *Ukimwi mbaya* – AIDS is bad
> *Tumia condom* – use a condom
> *Ukipata Gīkūyū, tumia moja* – if you get a Gīkūyū, use one
> *Ukipata Mmeru, tumia mbili* – if you get a Meru, use two.
> (Goes up to seven, for Borana)
> *Woi, lakini Jaluo, nyama kwa nyama* – but for a Luo, skin to skin[16]
> (don't use any)

The song is in tandem with perceived sexual stereotypes amongst the different communities in Kenya, which form an interesting research topic[17], beyond the scope of the chapter. But the stereotypes are couched in such ridiculous comments, e.g. *Ukipata Kalenjin, tumia sita* (if you get a Kalenjin girl, use six condoms!!) a different number for each community. But for the Gīkūyū, where most of *Mūgithi* artistes hail from, the association of their ethnic roots with normalcy (using just one) is telling. A different *Mūgithi* artiste, Mike Rua perpetuates the same sexual stereotypes of the different communities in Kenya:

> The Gīkūyū women are liked because of their agility in lovemaking
> The Luo women because of the large bosom
> The Luyha women because of their strong leg calves
> The Kamba women because of their sweetness.

This precisely is what Homi Bhabha (1983:37)says about stereotypes in the colonial discourse:

> ... [T]he stereotype is a form of knowledge and identification that vacillates between what is always in place, already known and something that must be anxiously repeated.

In line with this, it is crucial to note that most ethnic stereotypes in Kenya were propagated by the colonial authorities in their divide and rule policy. Macharia Munene (2000:2) quotes colonial apologist Elspeth

Huxley, '[S]he believed Gĩkũyũ were secretly cheeky, while Luos were lazy, Kambas sex maniacs and Somali and Maasai were trustworthy'. However, in post-colonial Kenya, political discourse has always been couched in ethnic Othering, with a view of 'animalising the Other …[where] Kenyatta's ethno-cultural conclusion of the Luo fits Max Weber's notion of social closure' argues Atieno Odhiambo (2002:242). It is in 'othering' the other communities, that Morson and Emerson, (1990:91) argue that for 'an integral *self*, a tentative self-definition requires an *other*. To know oneself, to know one's own image in the world, one needs another's finalizing outsidedness'. Nuances of *othering* are clearly expressed in the songs during a *Mũgithi* performance.

By parodying important songs by other communities through corrupting the lyrics, they make these songs sound quite meaningless and ridiculous. This particular Luhya[18] song is telling:

Khulikhwerwa eying'ombe x3 - (we've been brought a cow -for dowry)
mulayiwa mama   - a beautiful cow
eying'ombe   - a cow
konanganimbara eying'ombe x3 - I sleep while thinking about the cow
mulayiwa mama   - a beautiful cow
eying'ombe   - a cow

This is a wedding song, celebrating the value of dowry in the community, which is paid in cows in this community, like many others. The *Mũgithi* musician, in Gĩkũyũ language, retains the beat but subverts the whole theme of the song, and uses it to rebuke his sister Wanjiri:

Ũrĩ mwega, no wĩ ng'ombe – you are so nice, but you are a cow
Wanjirũ wa maitũ- Wanjiri my sister
Ũrĩ ngombe – you are cow
Ũgũkamwo nũũ - who do you think is going to milk you?
Mwanĩrie waku no ta wa ngombe – you sound like a cow
Mũkinyũkĩrie waku no ta wa ng'ombe – you even walk like a cow
Nginya mahũngũ maku no ta ma ng'ombe- your legs are like a cow's hooves

It is in giving this important song such crude connotations[19] to satisfy its audience that one feels that the music might be insensitive to other cultures.

However, the same musicians distort lyrics of fellow Gĩkũyũ musicians giving them bawdy connotations, and they are not just limited to mimicking religious hymns and traditional songs of other communities.

This corruption of the following gospel song is almost similar to the one above. But in the same vein, it ends up making fun of the Luo community and their main economic activity; fishing. The original gospel version goes thus:

> *Njakĩra nyũmba Mwathani*- help me build my house Lord[20]
> *Njakaga ĩkamomoka* –whenever I try, it keeps falling apart
> *Nĩngeretie maita maingĩ* – I have tried several times,
> *Itarĩ nawe ndingĩhota* – but without you I cannot make it.

Then, the corrupted verse by Salim Junior:

> *Njakĩra nyũmba Mwathani* -help me build my house Lord
> *Njakaga ĩkamomoka*- whenever I try, it keeps falling apart
> *Jaluo irageria gwaka* –When the Luo try to build theirs
> *Thamaki ikamomora* –the fish demolish them
> *Thamaki ciageria gwaka* –when the fish try to build theirs
> *Jaluo ikamomora* – the Luo demolish the houses

The above song is couched in political overtones and symbolisms. It signifies the political tensions that have always been there between the Luo and the Gĩkũyũ communities in Kenya from the time of Kenyatta and Jaramogi Odinga's conflicts immediately after independence. Building a house here denotes ascendancy to the highest political office in the land, the presidency. Though clothed in humour, the well-peddled stereotypes amongst the different Kenyan communities are quite explicit in most of the songs in *Mũgithi* performances.

But what we might call stereotypes again are comments of day-to-day happenings among ordinary people. As Stokes (1994:97) aptly argues, 'performance doesn't simply convey cultural messages already known, it reorganizes and manipulates everyday experiences of social reality, blurs, elides, ionizes and sometimes subverts commonsense categories and markers'. During the drought experienced in 1994, a small boy is said to have died of food poisoning in the Eastern province of Kenya, where in an effort to save himself from hunger, devoured the flesh of a dead dog. When this incidence came up in the press, it recorded in most Kenyans minds. A stereotype hitherto attributed to the Kamba people is that they eat dog meat. Thus, Mike Murimi's corruption of Kakai Kilonzo's song makes fun of this community and their tendency to consume dog meat.

What this chapter argues is that ethnic feelings and biases, as expressed in these songs, are not just interesting relics of a past, but live on in the cultural repertoire of present-day Kenya and form part of the perspective through which Kenyans view contemporary events. In fact, quite often, elements of the cultural legacy that are at best ethnocentric come to influence reactions and interpretations of current events.

The song below emanates from the out-of-the ordinary marriage between 67-year-old widow Wambui Otieno[21], a Gĩkũyũ woman and a 27-year-old man Mbugua, in mid - 2003. Wambui had been married to top lawyer SM Otieno, a Luo, who died in 1986. Cultural differences between herself and her husband's community created tension and a protracted legal battle on where to inter his remains. She finally lost the case and had remained single, and detached from her husband's community, until this marriage in 2003, to a fellow tribesman, Mbugua. The *Mũgithi* artists have dramatized this in a corruption of Suzzane Owiyo's song *Kisumu 100*, released for Kisumu city's centennial celebrations:

> *Haiyayee teraathianee Kisumu* -Haiyayee take me to go and see Kisumu
> *Kisumu ber Kisumu* - Kisumu is good
> *Teraadhianee kisumu* Kisumu take me to go and see Kisumu
> *Ndegeaidhoterawinam* –I'm boarding a plane to take me to the lake
> *Aidhomeliterawi got* –I'm boarding a ship to take me to the hills
> *Anadwarokendaongeng'amatera* - I want to do this by myself, no one is taking me[22]

Then the corruption of the song:

> *Haiyayee gũtirĩ njamba Gĩthumo* –haiya ii, there is no hero in Kisumu
> *Gũtirĩ njamba Gĩthumo* – there is no hero in Kisumu
> *Nĩthiĩte kinya Gĩthumo*– I have gone up to Kisumu
> *Kũrora kana kwĩ njamba*– to check whether there is a hero
> *No gũtirĩ njamba*– but there is no hero

This is in line with what Wambui herself said after the marriage, "Tell Nyalgunga people that I have gone forever... I am now married to a Gĩkũyũ from Gilgil. They should look for another Wambui!"[23] The musician picks cue from here, when they corrupt it and say 'there is no hero in Kisumu', probably to tame Wambui! Again, in relation to the protracted legal battle (over where the remains of the late S.M Otieno were to be interred) between Wambui and her husband's UmiraKager clan in 1986, the song can be read as a ridicule of the clan, which in spite of emerging victors in the Kenyan High Court and in the Court of Appeal, could not however contain Wambii as subject to Luo customary practice forever. Young Mbigua signifies the archetypical Gĩkũyũ riding roughshod over their bitter political rivals, the Luo.[24]

This takes us back to the issue of 'Othering' discussed above. The political differences between the Gĩkũyũ and the Luo in Kenya have over the years shaped the politics of the day in Kenya. Worth noting though is that KANU, the ruling party immediately after independence, and the loose coalition NARC, the opposition party which wrenched power from KANU after over four decades were both hinged on some unity between these two major ethnic communities in Kenya.

However, as stressed earlier, *Mũgithi* performance, despite concerning itself with ethnic stereotypes of other communities has managed to attract people from all walks of life, creeds and religions. Much as it is a Gĩkũyũ, urban phenomenon, the diverse audience and wide-ranging themes, beats and rhythms bring out the carnivalesque nature of the performance. While dealing with ethnic stereotypes, *Mũgithi* injects senses of humour and laughter in otherwise serious subjects. One can argue that in the performance, there is triumph over the official and the formal especially in the themes. Humour and laughter are main ingredients of the *Mũgithi* performance. Sexual explicitness couched in humour creates a free atmosphere for indulging in such thematic concerns. As Powell and Paton (1988: 126) argue, the use of humour itself constitutes a stylistic strategy, as well as a means of 'distancing the unpleasant, unpredictable or boring parts of our lives from our "real selves" by regarding them with less seriousness'. This in one sense can be seen as having a subversive effect on the dominant structure of ideas, thus representing a triumph of informality over the formal. Powell and Paton contend that humour 'contains resistance as well as expresses it' (p. 127).

Both control and resistance can be seen as converse relations between the virtuous and the pernicious. Of course, this depends on the perspective that one takes in this relationship. In phenomenological terms, it might make sense to dissolve control and resistance altogether, to recognise that irrespective of social location, life consists of organising experience in such a way that our sense of it makes us feel comfortable in balancing these two social forces. Life consists essentially of 'constantly negotiating our understandings with other people, establishing and maintaining by social controls and resistances our own virtue and those of our kind and the immorality and irrationality of others' (Powell and Paton, 1988:99). The humour, especially in stereotypes, 'reinforces our cultural distinctiveness by placing our shared practices into question' (Nyairo, 2005:8). The stereotypes, however, are desacralized and turned into complex idioms of laughter about imposed boundaries, be they ethnic, class or gender.

The humour evoked in the *Mũgithi* performance is both a means of laughing at others as well as laughing at everybody and at what they represent. This fits quite well with Bakhtinian's (1968:11) sense of carnival laughter, where it is not an individual reaction to some isolated comic event:

> Carnival laughter is the laughter of all people... it is directed at all and everyone, including the carnival and the participants. The entire world is seen in its droll aspect, in its gay relativity ... This laughter is ambivalent; it is gay, triumphant and at the same time mocking, deriding. It asserts and denies. It buries, it relives. Such is the laughter of the carnival.

Whereas ethnicity has been a serious political problem in Kenya, the use of the ethnic stereotypes in a humorous way to a multi-ethnic audience that characterizes *Mũgithi* performances depicts that the laughter 'builds its own world versus the official world, ...its own state versus the official state' (Bakhtin, 1965:88). It is this laughter that 'destroys all pretense of extra temporal meaning and unconditional value of necessity. It frees human consciousness, thought and imagination for new potentialities', (Bakhtin, 49).

The leaders as seen above manipulate ethnicity to their own ends. In the performance, this is celebrated where there is 'temporary suspension of the entire official system with all the prohibitions and hierarchic barriers' (Bakhtin, 89). The free-for-all atmosphere creates a sort of an ephemeral egalitarian and bohemian society, free from the real life ethnic differences. Like carnival, it is a performance where 'no one is outside, and nothing ever reaches a whole image ... it does not acknowledge any distinction between actors and spectators', (Morson and Emerson, 1990:92). When the musicians call for a response from the crowd, when people from different identities merge together in one, the divisions between spectators and actors are clearly diminished.

The differences in cultures is, however, emphasised in what is termed below as cultural or theme nights.1998 in Kenya saw the birth of what is termed as 'theme nights', a new entertainment phenomenon. A more fitting term would be cultural nights. At the up market Panafric Hotel in Nairobi, different Kenyan communities on different nights meet to engage themselves in cultural activities where music from the communities accompanied by the traditional foods and drinks is the order of the day. It is also a chance for the community to showcase its upcoming music talents to its members. They have existed in different names for the diverse communities; *MaloMalo* night for the Luo, *Bango* night for the coastal people, *Mūgithi* night for the Gīkūyū among others. It has been described as 'the meeting of the village and the city'. According to the progenitor of the phenomenon, 'many executives are too busy to travel upcountry to enjoy traditional music and dishes as often as they would like to, the village comes to them, giving them a taste of the life they yearn for. Here there is no class, no etiquette. One can dance holding one's stomach, bottoms, leg or knee with noeyebrows being raised. Above all, it creates a sense of belonging' (Obara: 2003).

For the Gīkūyū night to be labelled as *Mūgithi* night clearly spells out that despite the cosmopolitanism that goes with it, it is still an ethnic endeavour. Though, the trend now among all these theme nights is changing, because people show up at functions for other communities other than theirs to get a taste of different cultures.

Talking of the impact of the song-narrative in creating bonds among a community, Ruth Finnegan (1970:285) in her seminal study of oral literature in Africa argues:

One of the best examples of the use of songs for secret propaganda is the hymns [that were] used by the Mau Mau in Kenya in the early 1950s. This movement, part political, part religious was banned by government, and yet largely by means of these songs, was able to carry out active and widespread propaganda among the masses in Kenya.

The *Mūgithi* performance invoked some of the Mau Mau lyrics in the late 1990s and early 2000 provided patrons a forum to protest against Moi's suppression and economic marginalization especially of the Gīkūyū community[25], much as they did during colonialism. Political themes have dominated the entire performance with the artist actively engaging the audience through call-response techniques. This underlines the collective spirit in which most of these songs seek to invoke. The corruption of popular gospel songs has been evident, but the performer also has recreated songs that were sang during the Mau Mau period making them more relevant to contemporary situations. Such *Mūgithi* performances, heavily laden with political messages and strong appeal to Gīkūyū nationalism was possible in Thika prior to the 2002 elections, and other towns with a predominantly Gīkūyū setting.

The recourse to the Mau Mau period songs, like *Twathiaga Tūkenete* (we used to travel happily) might also link the performance to the proscribed Mūngīkī movement, a proscribed politico-religious group that is mostly seen as a neo Mau Mau movement. But it also asserts ethnic pride of the Gīkūyū. In this particular song, the musician invokes the "House of Mūmbi' tag:

> *Ona wathiī Nairobi, tūrī o kuo* – If you go to Nairobi, we are there
> *Ũthiī Narok, Baringo, Kabartonjo tūrī o kuo* - Even Narok, Baringo, Kabartonjo
> *Nyūmba ya Mūmbi twīyūmīrīrie* - House of Mūmbi, let's talk courage
> *Gūtirī handū tūtarī* -We are everywhere.

Mention of Baringo and Narok is crucial. The former president hails from Baringo, and Narok was one of the sites of ethnic cleansing, where a 'post-election attack on Kikuyus who voted against the ruling party (KANU), took place in October 1993. The orgy of violence left 30 people dead and over 30,000 others displaced' (Kagwanja, 2003:12). The musician here expresses hope and determination, and 'an optimistic belief in total emancipation'. The song thus becomes a form of 'hope-therapy' (Muhoro, 1997:115). There is also a very explicit expression of Gĩkũyũ nationalism and pride.

The evocation of the Mau Mau struggle here becomes symbolic and a metaphor of the realities in present-day Kenya. The reference to freedom fighters goes beyond an interest in imparting historical information and reconstructs the struggle as a 'myth which ordinary people would wish to 'impose' on reality, and to have it become the 'truth' and 'natural' – different from its official version' (Gecau, 1997:156).

Mũgithi in evoking songs that were sang during the Mau Mau struggle, is involved in the narration of the nation, in this case the Gĩkũyũ nation, described by Stuart Hall (1992:293) as a 'set of stories, images, landscapes, scenarios, historical events, national symbols and rituals which stand for or represent the shared experiences, sorrows and triumphs and disasters which give meaning to the nation'. The *Mũgithi* artists liken the situation in Kenya in the 1990s under Moi to the trying moments of the Kenyan nation in the 1950s under the colonialist. The rise of the politico-religious Mũngĩkĩ sect among the Gĩkũyũ in the 1990s was modeled along the Mau Mau activities in the 1950s.

Linking *Mũgithi* with Mũngĩkĩ might be problematic. While Mũngĩkĩ may be seen as a peasant uprising for the youth, '*Mũgithi* and its classless nature is associated firmly with an urban middle class' (Mbugua, 2000), as seen mostly in the theme nights. But that doesn't mean that the performance does not employ symbolism and imagery that has overtones of ethnic chauvinism, as demonstrated in the above song.

Conclusion

However, this chapter steers away from the depiction of the ethnic identity as a disruptive force. Theorists have argued that ethnic identity is 'an ordinary aspect of selfhood and a basic social relation which has in the past provided a sense of relative autonomy from the centralizing ambitions of the postcolonial African State, moral community for cultural citizenship and the focal point of resistance against tyranny' (Kagwanja, 2003:4, Eyoh, 1999:273). What is referred to as 'moral ethnicity' differs significantly from 'political tribalism', which Berman and Lonsdale

(1992:462) argue, is as a result of the patron-client relationships in modern politics and has undesirable effects towards achieving unity in a nation.

Secondly, the chapter has attempted to show the dynamics of ethnicity especially in postcolonial Kenya. As Berman, Eyoh and Kymlicka (2004:4) argue, 'African ethnic groups are not univocal, and the content of culture and custom, as well as the boundaries of the communities remain matters of frequent conflict and negotiation'. Again, ethnicity should not be seen purely as a matter of culture and tradition, but also about competition for power and wealth, as the cartoon below exemplifies.

It is imperative to note that *Mūgithi* performance is couched in ambiguity, and that any attempt to try and analyze it without taking into cognizance the contributing factors that led to its rise would be insufficient. Whether the performance is just another show of ethnic chauvinism, cultural regeneration, or a political mobilization tool in this context depends on the particular moment of production. As argued in the first part of the chapter, clear indications of political conscietisation are evident. As we have analyzed the stereotypes and cultural aspect, what remains to be seen of *Mūgithi* performance is its relevance in the post-Moi era.

Figure 1

The above 2003 editorial cartoon from a Kenyan daily attempts to answer the question about the relevance of *Mūgithi* performance in post-Moi

Kenya. No longer a performance of the oppressed, with the ascension of Kibaki, (or is it the Gĩkũyũ into political power?), *Mũgithi* has come to be associated with the powers that be, especially in this cartoon. Will the discontent in the coalition government, make or break the 'cosmopolitan *Mũgithi?*' The cartoon is a clear explication of the politics after the 2002 elections. The house across the river symbolizes the center of power, The State House, where according to the cartoonist, the occupants there are enjoying the benefits of power, dancing to the *Mũgithi* songs. The gentlemen on the other side of the river are meant to be KANU politicians from Kiambu district (a Gĩkũyũ zone) who feel locked out of power, or the 'ethnic' center or axis of power, now under the Gĩkũyũ of Nyeri, symbolized by the President himself.[26] However, an analysis of *Mũgithi* performance in the post-Moi era remains a fertile area of research, which is beyond the scope of this study.

This chapter, therefore, has been an attempt in understanding the ideology of vernacular music, ethnicity and class and political tensions in Kenya. The analysis is crucial because it is the different cultural values from all Kenyan communities that constitute the Kenyan national culture. The challenge however for vernacular musicians is to integrate the specific cultures of the various communities into the national whole.

In this analysis, songs from three leading *Mũgithi* artistes in Kenya; Mike Rua, Mike Murimi and Salim Junior have been quoted. Discographic details of their works are hard to come by. The music is hardly played on radio stations in Kenya, and all of them perform live in various locations. However, this music is now available on copied tapes and compact discs, but with no details such as dates of recording and recording companies. Such informalities inform the study of *Mũgithi* performance.

The phenomenal success of the performance and the growing popularity has led to several other artists, not necessarily from the Gĩkũyũ community recording their own versions of *Mũgithi*. One example is Man Wanjohi and Wyre appearing for Ted Josiah in a 2002 production and Kayamba Africa in 2004. Salim Junior and Mike Murimi's renditions of other popular musicians' lyrics are regularly played on Gĩkũyũ FM stations, such as Kameme FM, Coro FM and Inooro FM. It is worth noting that these stations omit the bawdy and sexually graphic lyrics that epitomize the repertoire of *Mũgithi* performance.

Notes

1 Peter Parkes examines the dynamics of song performance in articulating personal group and collective identities among the Kalasha of Chitral in Northwest Pakistan. He explicates how song performance dramatizes a 'solidary moral community that appears expressly united in the face of external oppression as well as internal animosities'.

2 Daytona Nightclub on the fringes of Nairobi city is where artiste Salim Junior, a *Mūgithi* artiste, used to perform.

3 This line is subject to various interpretations. While people are holding each other's waist, there is the license in the performance for men and women to touch each other in a sexually suggestive manner. It might also serve caution for people to take care of their pockets or handbags in the event of pick pocketing. I appreciate Sophie Macharia for the latter interpretation.

4 *Unbwogable* was a song done by two hip-hop artistes, Joseph Oyoo and Julius Owino. The song, done in Dholuo and English, gained national fame, especially as the anthem for the opposition party, NARC in the 2002 general election in Kenya that saw the end of the 39-year reign of Kenya's independence party, KANU. However, the lyrics pay respect to leaders and artistes, past and present, from the Luo community in Kenya.

5 Notes Masolo (2000:372) '[m]ost ... performers do not only entertain; they are also able, and frequently they aim, to raise the awareness level of their audience by arousing in them the imaginative and emotive experiences towards social re-engagement in the form of collective identity'.

6 Commenting on the music termed as 'seditious' and "subversive" that circulated among a wide audience especially in the early 1990s, Angelique Haugerud (1995:29) argues that 'such forms became crucial weapons in active struggles for political transformation'. The banning of the music in public places had little or no effect. Popular music, so argues Haugerud, was somewhere beyond the reach of the state, as the proliferation of 'informal' performances in bars and night clubs took toll. It is in this light that I appreciate the *Mūgithi* performance.

7 Worth noting, various musicians from diverse ethnic groups, with music otherwise thought to be subversive suffered the same fate. This attack was not peculiarly directed to the Gīkūyū, but I quote Gīkūyū examples to suit the specifities of the chapter.

8 See Evan Mwangi's article 'Journal's Special Issue on Kenya Focuses on Culture' in the *Sunday Nation* October 19th, 2003 where he argues that the song was politicized, by the consumers though, as a statement against single-party politics.

[9] As has been argued in the previous chapter on urban identities and *Mūgithi,* the performance falls under what has been termed as 'bar productions' Ndigirigi (1999:90), where artistes have redefined the bar in urban centers as a space for performance. Most of the music again is never given airtime on most broadcasting stations. In this context, the informality of *Mūgithi* refers to its performance within places of recreation, and hence its association with leisure, though at a deeper level, as this chapter agues, the performance becomes a vital component in the service of identity.

[10] Nairobi, in both the 1992 and 1997 elections remained an opposition orbit with KANU the then ruling party garnering a very low percentage as compared to Ford-Asili and DP. As Kimani Njogu argues, the politics of Central Province, (a traditionally opposition zone during Moi's era) affect the politics of the capital city mainly because of its proximity' p. 398. See Kimani Njogu's 'The Culture of Politics and Ethnic Nationalism in Central Province and Nairobi' (2001).

[11] Swahili for 'upcountry people' but has derogatory meanings when used by the indigenous coastal communities.

[12] Just like the ethnic clashes in the Rift Valley, the violence against upcountry people was a consciously instigated political effort to try and influence the outcome of 1997 general elections.

[13] Mwangi (2003) cautions against the tendency among scholars to overemphasize on the 'transformative' power of popular culture. We need to cast a suspicious gaze at popular culture because its products can be a conduit of stereotypes, especially against ethnic communities, women and other marginalized members of the society'.

[14] Ethnicity in Kenya, just like most former colonies in Africa can be attributed to the colonial legacy where the colonial powers had the ability to leave colonies whose people were divided along ethnic lines for them to continue having strong holdings on their former colonies. 'in the colonial state, they had struggled to have the colonial subjects united in the service of colonialism and yet remain divided when it came to promoting the political and economic interests of the colonized' argues Macharia Munene (2000). However, the consequent governments of Kenyatta and Moi, and more recently Kibaki cannot be absolved of the same blame of perpetuating ethnicity for political survival in the postcolonial Kenya. See also Carol Sicherman in *Race and Class* 37.4 (1996:63).

[15] Macharia Gaitho, 'Swelling Phobia for Big Tribes: Love and Hate have Defined Relationship with Gikuyu, Luo' in *Moi: End of an Era*, a special supplement of the *Daily Nation*, 24th December 2002.

[16] Skin-to-skin, makes a mockery of the Luo ethnic community's avoidance of male circumcision, a derogatory indictment which has often been applied when, what Cohen and Odhiambo (1992:15) call the 'reconvening of the old persisting struggles between the Luo and the Gīkūyū in Kenyan national life' surfaces.

[17] For a detailed analysis of different stereotypes among Kenyan communities, see Phyllis Nyambura's article, 'The Good, the Bad and the Ugly.' *Saturday Nation*, Online Edition. *December 27th 2003.*

[18] The wording of the song may be different, since the Luhya community comprises of different dialects. I am indebted to Leontyne Wamukoya for this translation and interpretation of the song.

[19] Despite the gender insensitive nature of such a song, the setting of the *Mũgithi* performance obscures such gendered readings, and both men and women alike are so engrossed in the revelry, in a 'free for all' mode where all inhibitions are cast aside.

[20] The implied meaning is 'help me be steadfast in my faith, Lord, for I keep backsliding'

[21]Wambui-Otieno-Mbugua is a well known personality and occupies a significant place in the Kenyan social imaginary, partly because, 'of the prominent and outspoken roles she has played and adopted in Kenyan political life, and principally as a result of ordinary Kenyans' absorption in the saga surrounding the burial of her husband SM Otieno in the mid-1990s' (Cloete, 2002:12-13). To propel her further into the national limelight was her wedding in 2003 to a 27-year-old man, Mbugua. Musicians, comedians, like Redykyulass comedy group have picked on Wambui as a theme in their art. Emily Nyagithiĩ's assistance in providing some of the recordings of Redykyulass shows on Wambui's wedding is appreciated.

[22] Translation by Dina Adhiambo Ligaga.

[23] A Nyatiti player, Ogwang' k'Okoth in 1987, (quoted in D.A Masolo's article, 'Presencing the Past and Remembering the Present: Social Features of Popular Music in Kenya'. 2000: 386) composed a song highlighting the legal tussle between Wambui Otieno and the UmiraKager clan over where to inter the remains of S.M Otieno. The song I quote above from the *Mũgithi* artist seems like a rejoinder to Ogwang's song. It denotes how songs speak to each other over different historical moments.

[24] I am indebted to Joyce Nyairo for this insight.

[25] Kimani Njogu notes, 'Central Province *[predominantly inhabited by the Gĩkũyũ]* had seen a systematic decline in the social and economic spheres since the 1980s. The Moi regime had systematically worked to dislocate and neutralize its hold in the national arena, inherited from the Kenyatta era ' (2001:382). [Emphasis mine]

[26] During Kenyatta's reign, his henchmen vowed that the power would never cross River Chania, a geographic feature that divides two distinct groups of the Gĩkũyũ community; the Kiambu Gĩkũyũ and the Nyeri Gĩkũyũ. One might argue that these are the two different ridges Ngũgĩ wa Thiong'o talks about in his book, *The River Between*. This editorial cartoon came after Kibaki visited the Kiambu district in a view of extending an olive branch to a people who overwhelmingly voted against him in the 2002 elections.

CONCLUSION

Music and Society: The Consummate Marriage

This body of research has been an analysis of the Gĩkũyũ music produced during the 1990s, but has also interrogated why a particular postcolonial moment operates to bring forth particular forms of cultural production. Renaissance in cultural production has been borne out of the complex politics of nation building in postcolonial Kenya, especially in the 1990s, the period under review.

This study has constantly argued that music has been a crucial aspect of everyday living. It has further claimed that music goes beyond the expected realm, as a tool of entertainment, to being a commentary and a response of day-to-day happenings. It is, however, not an innocent commentary, but in this case, as a means of bringing people together, especially in suffering. As has been evident in most of the music discussed, the confraternity in suffering and a hope for a better future have been major themes that have come up. All this then constitutes what has consistently been referred to as the politics of everyday life, which goes beyond the macro nature of state politics, to the micro-narratives that inform the daily experiences of the people.

As this study has attempted to show, the music produced by these popular musicians does not exist in a void, but that it is also influenced by the societal experiences. There is, however, a symbiotic relationship between music and society, for instance, when musicians form part of the popular speech. Growing up in the village, musician Joseph Kamarũ used to be a reference point especially when elderly people were commenting on the moral degradation. Kamarũ's *Ndanuko cia Mĩtahato* was often quoted when castigating people who have grown up in urban centres and have since lost touch with their culture. Most of these conversations would normally start in a formulaic sense; *Ota ũrĩa mũini Kamarũ augaga* ... (Just like Kamarũ the musician says in his song...). In such instances therefore, this research argues that music and society exist alongside each other.

Through an analysis of both the lyrics and the context within which the music is created and received, the argument has been that music should be approached as part of a more discontinuous process in which cultural traditions are continuously remade and new hybrid identities are created. Studying popular music thendoes not have to simply involve following the linear communication of musical messages from musicians to audiences. Instead, it is through examining the process of articulation in which particular sounds or lyrics seek out and connect with particular audiences, as is the case with the *Mũgithi* performance.

From the introductory chapter, several deductions have been made. Firstly, there is recognition that the growth of contemporary music in Kenya, and in particular Gĩkũyũ music, is as a result of the interaction between the local and the foreign, the outside and indigenous regional sounds. The music is dynamic and is bound to produce new trends and genres in future with the increased interaction, with the understanding that popular culture is free, dynamic and ever-changing. There is a constant interplay between the local/foreign, traditional/modern, official/ unofficial, ethnic/national categories. The common denominator, however, is that the music deals with all aspects of everyday lives of the people. The contentionhere then is that music should be studied as a component in the daily lives and experiences of the society.

With the background of the 1990s in Kenya, the second chapter has shown how songs respond to certain situations. Taking a few case studies of Gĩkũyũ musicians, this study has explicated how the decade in question was a dislocating moment for Kenyans, but how it also provided ammunition for the musicians in their socio-political commentaries. However, taken independently of the realities of the 90s, the meanings of the songs might be different altogether.

Chapter Three demonstrated ways in which the intersection between politics and music 'foregrounds the ever present negotiation between the individual and the group, and the contradictions that arise because group actions entail the self-styling of many individuals' (Allen, 2004:8). The chapter showed how the definition of patriotism depends on who is in power, and what constitutes treason might actually be the opposite. The conclusion, however, is that the state has permeated every other aspect of its subjects (especially composers and musicians) and interferes with their day-to-day living.

The inference in the fourth chapter is that music is not always a site of subversion, but that the moment of production of a certain piece plays a crucial role. With a detailed analysis of Joseph Kamarū, the famed Gīkūyū musician, the chapter has indicated that the musician is always caught up in the ambiguities and contradictions of the postcolony. Kamarū's character vacillates between two extremes; as a praise singer and as a critic to the same regime in a period of six years! However, another deduction has been that living is always about negotiating and re-negotiating identities as well as shifting goalposts. As with the popular saying, it depends on which side of the musician's bread is buttered.

Chapters Five and Six have delineated ways in which *Mūgithi* performance, a relatively new genre of Gīkūyū music, is a crucial site for negotiation and re-negotiation of the multiple forms of identities in the postcolony. The politics of everyday life are as complicated as the politics of the postcolony. It is in the performance that both the musician and the audience 'perform identities', as the situations dictates. Traditional forms of music find their way in modernised urban centres while gospel lyrics entertain revellers in a nightclub or a bar; a member of the Kamba community would sing and dance joyously to a song stereotyping his people while sang in Gīkūyū language and so on, goes the performance. The performance blurs boundaries between urban/rural, men/women, secular/religious and in one moment, the audience becomes one happy family. This is what the study has referred to as the 'performance of identities' because outside the performance, these said differences are dominant in everyday life in such great magnitudes. The carnival nature of the performances injects humours in otherwise serious subjects as way of laughing at others, as well as laughing at everybody else.

It is in these discussions, as outlined in the chapters, where the research insists that music and everyday living are inextricably linked; in a way that music cannot be discussed independent of the extra-textual world, which is the real world we are living in. A study of the society as well will provide a template on which to comprehensively research on its music. This is what is herein referred to as the consummate marriage between music and society.

Further research on the politics of everyday living in music should take cognisance of these conclusions. Music in Africa, one would argue has provided alternative sites for contesting and subverting some of the repressions put in place by the ruling elite. This research has been a study of Gĩkũyũ music, to demonstrate how it operates within the framework of specific social, economic and political circumstances. The findings have shown how this music has helped define these very circumstances by providing the metaphors and idioms with which to better articulate these experiences. The argument has been that the study of the music clearly articulates the complex and contradictory impulses that define the nation called by the contribution of popular culture in the last two decades or so as a major site of political and social negotiation in Africa.

Appreciating music as text offers new possibilities of studying music. This research has not been talking about the notes, sounds and the harmonic progressions of a piece. By studying music as a text, the study was mainly interested in the lyrics as explicated in the introductory chapter but also the context within which the music is performed. This investigation has been on how meaning, identities and values are negotiated, exchanged and dramatized in musical products.

In understanding popular music, the study veers from musicological perspectives whose main concern is in the processes, which are intrinsic, that is sonic, motional and visual. The study is more interested in the contextual processes. These are historical, social, cultural, political and biographical processes which are extrinsic to the musical event but 'which nonetheless imbue the event itself with meaning and significance for people' (Shepherd, 1991:196).[1]

Popular music, as Barber (1997:1) argues is the 'most protean, adaptable and transferable of the arts', because of its versatility and easy memorability. Musicians in expressing ideas about their ethnic communities are not involved in internal competition for control over the local resources amongst themselves unlike the ethnic elite, who are out to manipulate the tropes of kinship to negotiate the conditions of political representation and participation within the wider political system. Appealing to their audience, musicians espouse new ideas of thinking about citizenship. Despite talking about common problems affecting the whole nation, e.g., poor leadership, or economic difficulties, the specifity is always on their immediate community.

The fact that the vernacular music appeals only to a certain group (especially in lyrics), a polyglot society like Kenya will always find it hard to come to terms with the concept of national citizenship, even at this particular moment. Gĩkũyũ will think of themselves as Gĩkũyũ first, Kenyans second. No wonder, it is always 'our chance to eat', in every general election in Kenya, when communities decide that it is their turn for one of their son or daughter who is gunning for the presidential seat to lead the country.

There is further emphasis in the study that ethnic feelings and biases, as expressed in these songs are not just interesting relics of a past, but live on in the cultural repertoire of present-day Kenya and form part of the perspective through which Kenyans view contemporary events. In fact, quite often, elements of the cultural legacy that are at best ethnocentric come to influence reactions and interpretations of current events.

The past, according to the study, has been seen to offer a source of inspiration for most musicians. Joseph Kamarũ, Queen Jane and *Mũgithi* artists revert to traditional genres of Gĩkũyũ music namely *Mwomboko* and *Mũcũng'wa*. The recourse to Mau Mau lyrics by musicians points to the relationship between music and politics. The songs performed during the struggle served as a vehicle to mobilise as well as coalesce Kenyans and Gĩkũyũ people in particular against the colonialist. The fact that similar lyrics are replayed presently denotes a sense of continuity from the colonial to the postcolonial. Though not in such direct sense, political repression and disregard of people's interests by subsequent governments have continued unabated.

This study has also shown how musicians either copy or improvise the lyrics of the past in their present endeavours. *Mũgithi* artists go further when they offer renditions of other musicians outside the Gĩkũyũ community. The effect for *Mũgithi* performance is to attract divergent audiences, given that it is an urban phenomenon. Crucially, then, as this research has concluded, popular music in present day Kenya is a mixture of the local and the regional. The *benga* beat has antecedents from former Zaire.

As Nyairo and Ogude (2003: 385) have argued, ethnicity is one of the many sources of national character, of the attempts to form a distinctly unique sense of Kenyanness in such a polyglot, multi-ethnic state like Kenya. Continually reshaped by the intersection of local and external social, economic, political and cultural forces, the result in such a state is 'political systems which are ordered by overlapping and often conflicting notions of political community, principals of political representation and the moral basis for evaluating and contesting the legitimacy of political authority: one ethnically defined, and the other national and state-centred' (Eyoh, 2002).

Eyoh (2002) rightly argues that 'while the constellation of forces shaping patterns and outcomes of electoral competition has varied across societies, it is clear that the return of multi-party politics has led to an intensification of the politics of primary patriotism'. One would hasten to argue, from the above examples that this has been borne out of political repression in the one-party era. This goes further to explain the complexities of studying the interplay between popular music, ethnicity and patriotism in post colonial Kenya.

While theorizing about the various themes expressed in the music, we should not lose the other salient fact that music for the musician is a means of livelihood too, and not just a political or social commentary of the politics of everyday. The rise of gospel music amongst popular secular musicians, or inclusion of religious themes, in secular music attests to this. The study of gospel and religious music in Kenya forms a rich area of research enquiry, which was beyond the scope of this study. The ambiguities of musicians is necessitated by the fact that performers have always to contend with the double edged sword of both being needed and respected and at the same time deeply feared and mistrusted. In postcolonial Africa 'the mistrust towards the musician as a person making his living from an improper walk of life, is prevalent'. (Palmberg and Kirkegaard, 2002:10) This same can be said of Kenya.

Musicians have always been open to manipulations by the state to further its political agenda. The case of Muungano choir as was argued in chapter three, clearly demonstrates that music is not always a site of subversion. Depending on the moment of production, a song can either be read to be subversive or allied to the hegemonic structure. It would be interesting in future studies to evaluate and analyze the *Mūgithi* performance as well as other musical productions by Gĩkũyũ musicians in the period after the 2002 elections. The fact that that this study accentuates is that ethnicity in Kenya, which plays a major role in the politics of the day, affects the music as well.

The rise of vernacular stations in the multi-party era has opened up new spaces for musicians. With the production of music being less censored, critical music has ventured into the airwaves. This has given rise to a new forum for engaging in politics of the day. Politics generally have left the podium and filtered down to the common man on the streets. Live performances in nightclubs and restaurants have emerged as new spaces for engaging in politics. Apart from popular music, other popular cultural productions include vernacular theatre, comedies and paintings, all outside the highbrow culture of previous years.

In everyday life music can be hard to distinguish from other cultural elements. It is not easy to discuss music without taking into consideration how the dance is performed and how the lyrics relate to social, cultural or political events and happenings.

The current politics of identity, usually stressing one's independence and self-supporting qualities is evidenced by the proliferation of popular arts. However, the argument in this research throughout has been that the cultural practices of public performances play a crucial role as local and global vehicles to '(re)produce, contest, transform, deconstruct and adapt to varying forms of authority' (Boeck 1996:100).

The music discussed so far is crucial in playing and negotiating identities. One fact is that the music plays a crucial role in the countryside as well as in the urban and diasporic centers. This is due to the spread of modern media primarily the radio 'but it is also a continuation of the exchange between migrating peoples and in this way displays the dynamics of musical culture' (Palmberg and Kirkegaard, 2002:14).

Although there is a subtle critique of the regime embedded in the cultural politics in the Gĩkũyũ music, we can read this not so much as an attitude of contest, resistance or conflict with the state. Rather, it is an attempt 'to use the state, collaborate with it and invade its space in order to further, among other things their political agenda' (De Boeck 1996:99).

Ethnicity, identity and music discussions in this study, however, are not lost to the fact that identities are always shifting everywhere depending on the surrounding circumstances. Again, the music cannot be said to be appealing to a whole ethnic group, there is no single homogenous ethnic group. There are always class and gender categorisations, amongst others. The music too should be approached with care whilst studying it; it's always necessary to look at the motives behind the production, and the ideas of audiences and how the music is received.

Notes

[1] Shepherd (1991:190) argues that if musicology fails to recognise the inherently social nature of music, the discipline fails as well to 'recognise the possible specificities of music as a social form'. This way, it might end up 'condemning itself to an even more peripheral position in the academic world than it presently occupies'

Jane Nyambura (Queen Jane)
1965- 2010

Jane Nyambura, popularly known by her stage name, Queen Jane, passed away on the 30th of June 2010 in a Nairobi hospital in Kenya. Some of her music was part of my research inquiry and I felt compelled to write a tribute to her. A version of this tribute was published in the *Saturday Nation* newspaper in Kenya on July 10th 2010.

Queen Jane: A Tribute to the Voice of the Voiceless

The stub on Wikipedia about the late Jane Nyambura, better known as Queen Jane, is not representative of the space that this fallen heroine of Gĩkũyũ popular music has occupied in the Kenyan social imaginary and the cultural scene. Born Jane Nyambura, 45 years ago, Queen Jane's stature as the leading Gĩkũyũ popular musician will remain etched in the memories of many a fan of her *benga* beat.

It has been difficult from the various press reports in Kenya to exactly verify her place of birth, but all are in agreement that she was born in the then Murang'a district, which has now been split into various districts. This is an indication that she was the undisputed queen of Gĩkũyũ music, not only in the area, but nationally as well. When the national broadcaster's website wrongfully stated that she was born in Gatanga, this aroused in me my earliest memories of Queen Jane.

Regarded as the home of Gĩkũyũ music, the galaxy of stars from Gatanga have never failed their fans from the division, where the constantly perform gigs in the area. In the mid-1980s to the 1990s, Queen Jane would accompany musicians from Gatanga, like Wamumbe and John Ndichu, in their tours in the constituency. When she performed in Gatura's Chini Club, at the Tarmac End Inn, Antony Kamau from Houston, Texas, who hails from the area, remembers one day with nostalgia, when Queen Jane performed in Gatura, in the late 1980s. 'It was my first time ever to come face to face with a Kenyan celebrity'. Despite many years in the USA, he still remains a fan of Queen Jane's music.

I recall the excitement of my elder brothers' faces whenever they would attend the regular live performances in my village, Gatura, one of the major stop of most of the Gatanga musicians. Being roughly 10 years in the mid-1980s, I could only understand their excitement much later when I encountered her music in my research endeavours.

It is extremely difficult to talk about Queen Jane and her music in isolation. Right from where she started, with Simon Kihara, better known as Musaimo, to the time of her demise, Queen Jane has commanded respect from musicians and fans alike. In her music as well, this spirit of collaboration has been evident with her overt mention of fellow musicians in her songs. In business sense, these would be her competitors, but this goes to show her great personality in the music world.

In fact, one musician, Timona Mburu of the *Wĩ Sumu* fame, composed a song in honour of Queen Jane after her marriage to James Kariuki in 2001, saying that those who have eyed her should know that she is queen of Kariuki now. Queen Jane herself did a song thanking all those musicians and radio personalities mostly from Kameme FM, who attended her wedding.

Most of contemporary musicians Gĩkũyũ musicians have been products of Queen Jane's magnanimity. Renowned *Mũgithi* one-man guitarists, Mike Murimi, Salim Junior and Mike Rua started off first with Queen Jane's group QueenJa Les Les Band. Queen Jane too mentored her younger sisters Lady Wanja and Princess Aggie, as well as Dr Michuki her brother, who are now musicians in their own right.

Having launched her career at the tender age of 19 with Musaimo in 1984, Queen Jane will be remembered as the trendsetter of Gĩkũyũ secular music by women artists. Apart from the Nyakinyua dancers in the 50s and the 60s, the Gĩkũyũ woman voice was largely muted, and the woman artists were just but accompanying artists. Roman Warigi, a guru of Gĩkũyũ music in the 50s and 60s used to record with the sister Muthoni, but he carried the by-line alone. Joseph Kamaru also used to sing with his sister Catherine, but Kamaru always got the credits.

It was only in the 1970s that Elizabeth Nyambene and Julia Lucy opened the way for the recognition of women singers. But these two artists were purely gospel artists.

As things began to change in secular groups, it became increasingly common to hear of Kamaru Sisters, and Chania Sisters (in the case of Peter Kigia's Chania River Boys Band). Others included Kihara Sisters (of the Mbiri Young Stars) and Karura Sisters (of Karura Brothers). The lifting of the veil off the female voice increased both the volume and the quality of productions, while at the same time helping to expose female musicians to the music scene. Now, one could hear female artistes belting out witty responses to the lyrical accusations that male singers had been levelling against Kenyan womanhood.

And in the 1980s, Queen Jane entered the fray, but this time giving the female voice the prominence it duly deserved. Queen Jane was a talented composer, and competently fused the old and the new, both in terms of lyrics and tunes. Like other Gĩkũyũ artists, Queen Jane inculcated the traditional forms into her popular music. In her initial recordings, she would include the traditional folk form *Mũcũngw'a* within her contemporary *benga*. Her albums covers then featured her dressed in traditional attire of the Gĩkũyũ community; in *mũthuru*, which was a skirt made of skin, and huge earrings, known as *hang'i*. Quite befitting an attire for the queen of Gĩkũyũ music!!

Where the female perspective was largely suppressed, or represented by the male Gĩkũyũ artist, Queen Jane's intervention as a secular singer was timely. In most of her songs, she has directly attacked the patriarchal hegemony. Her song, *Arũme Majini* (Men are Ghosts) was inspired by an increase in the number of rape and defilement cases in Kenya.

This is the same theme echoed in her hit song *Mũthuuri Teenager*, and *Guka Nĩndarega*, (I refused to be married to an old man/grandfather) where she scathingly attacks 'sugar daddies'; old men that trick young schoolgirls into relationships, which end up as soon as they start, consequently ruining the young girls' lives.

Some male fans have felt that she has been too strong in her condemnation against their own. Sam Ngigi, in Johannesburg South Africa feels that her choice of words is rather harsh, especially against men. In one of her songs, Queen Jane stresses that *Arũme nĩ Nyamũ* (Men are

Beasts), in taunting Casanovas, who jump from one lover to another with reckless abandon.

But Queen Jane was never apologetic about this, as she once declared that 'the fact that men are among my greatest fans simply means that I am telling the truth'. The above underlies the fact that musicians do not deal with issues that are out of this world, but actually the daily happenings.

However, her strong lyrics against men abuses have triggered off a continuous dialogue and interplay in gender and power relations in the Gĩkũyũ music. As Queen Jane castigates the behaviour of men in relationships, especially that of sugar daddies, as in her song *Nĩndarega Kũhikĩra Guka* (I refuse to be married to a grandfather), male Gĩkũyũ musicians seem to be offering responses. Sam Muraya's famous *Mama Kiwinya* scathingly attacks older women (better known as sugar mummies) who find comfort in young boys as their lovers. The same is evident in Joseph Kariuki's *Nyina wa Turera*, where he says that it's wrong for a woman of 40 years to date a young boy of 20.

This consistent dialogue between musicians across the gender divide has encapsulated the day-to-day realities in the society. The tensions in gender relations emanate from the myth of origin of the Gĩkũyũ people. Originally a matriarchal society, men revolted against the system and replaced it with a patriarchal one.

But far from the gender debate, her music has been well known for the social messages that they carry through. The music covers themes that are not only real but also easy to identify with. She is not only attacking men, but also wayward women, like the sweet-time girls who are out to cause mayhem to the family institution. In her song *Tũnua Baggy* (Loose mouths), she is not polite to gossips and rumour mongers, who are personified in female characters, Wangari and Wanjiku!

Her songs on love are rather on fulfilled love. Her songs *Ndĩmũnogu* (I am tired of waiting), *Mwendwa KK, Ndũraga Ngwetereire* (I have been Waiting for You) depict a lover who is running out of patience with a man who is taking forever to commit to the relationship. In the song, *Nyumbũrĩra,* (Confess to me), she implores her lover to take his stand sooner than later, instead of wasting time doing his calculations. At best, most of her songs on love are mostly sad love songs. In most of these songs, she is depicting herself as a victim, consequently earning sympathy from her audience and fans.

Some of her songs attest to the problems she has had to contend with in a career that is male dominated and where female musicians are easily mistaken for pros-titutes. In the song above, *Nyumbūrīra,* she is sad that the friends of her lover are discouraging him from continuing with the relationship simply because Queen Jane is a musician.

A running theme in all her music is the message to the youth to respect their parents. In the song *John Bull,* Queen Jane revisits the theme of rags-to-riches of the young man, John Ndegwa, but who later rejects his parents and changes his name to John Bull. She warns of the power of the curse of the poor parents whom he mistreats when he gets rich!

Queen's music, however, has been most notable in depicting the class consciousness. She didn't only take the responsibility of being the voice of the women, but also the voice of the voiceless. In one song, *Ndereba cia Matatū*, she valorises the work of *matatu* drivers, whom she says are as intelligent and useful in the society as any other professional. This led to her recognition by Matatu Welfare Association as the best Gīkūyū lady singer. She has also addressed the plight of orphans in her song *Mwana wa Ndigwa,* (The Orphan) and widows *Mūtumia wa Ndigwa.*

But the most telling one was the song *Hawkers,* in which she cries with them and also lashes out at the Nairobi City Council authorities. But a background to this song clearly shows that Queen Jane did not shy away from commenting on the injustices by the then government.

At the onset of the multi-party democracy in Kenya in the 1991, popular music and theatre were useful expressive forms which Kenyans use to voice their discontent at the excesses of the one-party regime. The Moi regime responded by being more stringent on cultural productions, banning plays and music. But artists and audiences alike found new avenues of expressing themselves away from the officialdom. Music with political content was played in bars and *matatus*. Hawkers became very instrumental in the sale and distribution of these cassettes, but were met with brutality from state officials, who arrested them, demolished their kiosks and some lost their lives.

Highlighting the plight of hawkers on Nairobi streets, Queen Jane in the song *Hawkers* offered a glimpse of these tribulations by hawkers, where, striving to free themselves from the shackles of unemployment, they are frustrated by the political dispensation of the day. State apparatus is exemplified by the Nairobi City Council *askaris* who endlessly harass the hawkers.

The musician illustrates the social stratum graphically and metaphorically when she queries the humanity of the *askaris*:

Andũ aya ngũria maciarirwo nĩ atumia /Kana nĩ nyamũ cia gĩthaka/ Kana nĩ rũciaro rũrĩa rwa Cain/Rworagire Habiri/Rũkĩrumwo nĩ Ngai - Are these people born of women? /or wild animals? Or are they descendants of Cain/who killed Abel/ And God cursed them?

The dehumanising act by the policemen on the hawkers goes beyond the social stratification. To the singer, it is not even an issue of class. She doesn't expect human beings to treat fellow humans in that regard. The spineless and ruthless character of the powers-that-be is laid bare.

Queen Jane's lament of the plight of the hawkers was symbolic of the many struggles that a great proportion of Kenyans went through during that time. Such lyrics offer critique to officialdom for the everyday problems of the non-elite listeners and elite listeners alike.

These thematic concerns are expressed in Queen Jane's masterly of the Gĩkũyũ language, and her choice of words clearly captures the idioms of everyday life amongst Kenyans. She doesn't shy away from being caustic while commenting on vices in the community. In her song, *John Bull*, she calls the young man *Kĩrimũ gĩkĩ* (you fool) for disrespecting his parents. Some of her titles carry oxymoron references, for example, *Mũthuuri Teenager* (Mzee teenager), or *Arũme nĩ Nyamũ* (Men are beasts). In a sarcastic attack to sugar daddies in the song, *Guka Nĩndarega,* she sings of a man who is as old as the soil/land (*mũthuuri mũkũrũ ta tĩĩri*). In the sad love songs, she talks of W*endo wa kĩbarũa* (Casual love), or *wendo wa ibango* (love in small measures), but drawing on idioms of the ordinary person in Kenya.

Despite having a relatively short entry on Wikipedia, the same cannot be said of her huge following on the video sharing network, *You Tube*. Her song, *Ndũraga Ngwetereire* (I have been waiting for you) has recorded over 210, 000 hits by the time of writing this piece. On record, this is the highest number of hits on any secular Gĩkũyũ song on You Tube to date. This is an interesting observation. Kenyans in the Diaspora regularly fall back to the Internet to access local music. Thus, this denotes that she has had a huge following outside Kenya as well.

Coincidentally, the song resonates with experiences of long distance relationships occasioned by Kenyans going abroad. These are the experiences that directly affect those in the Diaspora, (*rũraya*) and those that have been left back at home. Another sad love song, *Ndũraga Ngwetereire* expresses hope that even after the many years of physical separation, the fire of the love will keep glowing.

In her death, Queen Jane's music will continue to command a huge following. As Dr. Fred Mbogo of Moi University comments, 'what is reassuring is that her body of work which is quite large will continue to be played for a long time to come- because it seems to me to speak of life so passionately and objectively'. There is no better wording than this to sum up Queen Jane's life, music and her contribution to the Kenyan cultural scene.

BIBLIOGRAPHY

Adar, G. Korwa and Isaac Munyae. 'Human Rights Abuse in Kenya Under Daniel Arap Moi, 1978-2001'. *Africa Studies Quarterly* 5(1) 1, 2001.

Agawu, Kofi. 'Introduction' *Research in African Literatures* 32(2) 2001.

Agawu, Kofi. 'African Music as Text' *Research in African Literatures* 32(2) 2001.

Ajulu, Rok. ´The Left and the Question of Democratic Transition in Kenya: A Reply to Mwakenya´ in *Review of African Political Economy*, 22 (64) 1995.

Allen, Graham. *Intertextuality*. London and New York: Routledge, 2000.

Allen, Lara. 'Music and Politics in Africa' in *Social Dynamics* 30(2), 2004.

Allen, Lara. *Representation, Gender and Women in Black South African Popular Music*. Ph. D Thesis, University of Cambridge, March 2000.

Amran, Athman. 'Wambui Otieno 67, Weds 28-year-old Man' in *East African Standard*, July 19th 2003.

Anderson, Benedict. *Imagined Communities: Reflections on the Origin and Spread of Nationalism*. London: Verso, 1983.

Appadurai, Arjun. 'Patriotism and its Futures' in *Public Culture* 5(3), 1993.

Ashton, Dore. *Picasso on Art: A Selection of Views*. New York: The Viking Press, 1972.

Baily, John. 'The Role of Music in the Creation of an Afghan National Identity, 1923-73', in Martin Stokes, (Ed) *Ethnicity, Identity and Music: The Musical Construction of Place*. Oxford: Berg, 1994.

Bakari, Mohammed. 'Kenya Elections 2002: The End of Machiavellian Politics?', in *Alternatives: Turkish Journal of International Relations 1(4)*, 2002.

Bakhtin, Mikhail. *Rabelais and his World.*Cambridge, Mass: The M.I.T. Press, 1968.

Balliger, Robin. 'Politics', in *Key Terms in Popular Music and Culture*, Horner, Bruce and Thomas Swiss, Eds. Massachusetts: Blackwell Publishers Inc, 1999.

Barber, Karin. *Readings in African Popular Culture* Bloomington, Ind: International African Institute in association with Indiana University Press, 1997.

Barber, Karin. *West Africa Popular Theatre*. Bloomington, Ind., 1997.

Barber, Karin. 'Preliminary Notes on Audiences in Africa', in *Africa 67 (3)*, 1997.

Barber, Karin. 'Popular Arts in Africa', *African Studies Review 30(3)*, 1987.

Barra, G. *1000 Kikuyu Proverbs*. London: McMillan and Co. Ltd, 1990.

Barth, Fredrik (Ed). *Ethnic Groups and Boundaries: The Social Organization of Culture Difference*. Bergen-Oslo: UniversitetsForlaget, 1969.

Barz, Gregory. *Performing Religion: Negotiating Past and Present in Kwaya Music of Tanzania*. New York: Rodopi Publishers, 2003.

Bayart, Jean-Francois. *The State in Africa: Politics of the Belly*. London: Longman, 1993.

Bebey, Francis. *African Music: A People's Art*. London: Harrap, 1974.

Bellamy, William. 'Democracy in Kenya: Some Observations' in *Whitehall Papers* 62:1, 2004.

Bender, Wolfgang. *Sweet Mother: Modern African Music*. Chicago: University of Chicago Press, 1991.

Berman Bruce, Dickson Eyoh and Will Kymlicka. *Ethnicity and Democracy in Africa*. Oxford: James Currey, 2004.

Berman, Bruce and John Lonsdale. *Unhappy Valley: Conflict in Kenya & Africa*. London: James. Currey, 1992.

Bhabha, Homi. Ed. *Nation and Narration*. London: Routledge, 1990.

Bhabha, Homi. 'The Other Question' in *Screen*, 24:6, Nov-Dec1983.

Biko Steve. *I Write What I Like: A Selection of His Writings*. Aelfre Stubbs (ed) London: Heinemann, 1979.

Billy, Bergman. *African Pop: Goodtime Kings*. Poole: Blandford Press, 1985.

Blacking, J. 'Expressing Human Experience Through Music', in R. Byron (Ed.), *Music, Culture, and Experience: Selected Papers of John Blacking* (pp. 223–242). Chicago: University of Chicago Press, 1995.

Boeck, Filip de. 'Postcolonialism, Power and Identity: Local and Global Perspectives from Zaire', in Werbner, Richard and Terence Ranger, *(eds) Postcolonial Identities in Africa*. London and New Jersey: Zed Books, 1996.

Brodnicka, Monika, "When Theory Meets Practice, Undermining the Principles of Tradition and Modernity in Africa," *Journal on African Philosophy,* 2, 2003.

Brooks, A. *Post feminisms: Feminism, Cultural Theory and Cultural Forms*. London: Routledge. 1997.

Broughton, Simon Mark Ellingham and Richard Trillo, with Orla Duane and Vanessa Dowell. *World Music: The Rough Guide. Volume I*. London: Rough Guides, 1999.

Carter, E., Donald, J., and Squires, J. *Cultural Remix: Theories of Politics and the Popular* London: Lawrence & Wishart, 1995.

Chambers, Iain. *Urban Rhythms: Pop Music and Popular Culture*. London: Macmillan, 1985.

Chatterjee, Partha. *The Nation and Its Fragments: Colonial and Postcolonial Histories*. Princeton: Princeton University Press, 1993.

Chatterjee, Partha. *Nationalist Thought and the Colonial World: A Derivative Discourse?* London: Zed Books for the United Nations University, 1986.

Chernoff, John Miller. *African Rhythm and African Sensibility: Aesthetics and Social Action in African Musical Idioms.*Chicago: Chicago University Press, 1979.

Chirambo, Reuben Makayiko. '"Mzimuwa Soldier": Contemporary Popular Music and Politics in Malawi'. In: Englund, Harri (ed.). *A Democracy of Chameleons. Politics and Culture in the New Malawi.* Uppsala: NordiskaAfrikainstitutet, Blantyre: Christian Literature Association in Malawi (CLAIM/MABUKU),2002. pp. 103-122.

Clark, Jude. 'Urban Culture: Representations and Experiences in/of Urban Space and Culture', in *Agenda* 57, 2003. Source: Agenda, No. 57, Urban Culture (2003), pp. 3-10.

Cloete, Elsie Leonora. *Re-telling Kenya: Wambui Waiyaki Otieno& Mau Mau's Daughter*. PhD Thesis, University of the Witwatersrand, 2002.

Cohen, David William and E.S Atieno Odhiambo. *Burying SM: The Politics of Knowledge and the Sociology of Power in Africa.*London: J. Currey, 1992.

Connell, John and Chris Gibson. *Sound Tracks: Popular Music, Identity and Place*. London; New York: Routledge, 2003.

Conquergood, Dwight. 'Rethinking Ethnography: Towards a Critical Cultural Politics', in *Communication Monographs*, 58 (2), 1991.

Coplan, David, B. *In the Time of Cannibals: The Word Music of the Basotho People of South Africa*. Johannesburg: Witwatersrand University Press, 1994.

Coplan, David, B. *In Township Tonight!: South Africa's Black City Music and Theatre*. London: Longman, 1985.

Coplan, David, B. 'The Urbanisation of African Music: Some Theoretical Observations' in *Popular Culture 2*, 1982.

Enzensberger, Hans Magnus. 'Constituents of a Theory of the Media' in *Raids and Reconstructions*. London, 1976.

Erlmann, Veit. *Music, Modernity and The Global Imagination: South Africa and the West*. Oxford: Oxford University Press, 1999.

Erlmann, Veit. *African Stars: Studies In Black South African Performance.* Chicago: University of Chicago Press, 1991.

Euba, Akin. 'Text Setting in African Composition.' *Research in African Literatures* 32 (2), 2001.

Eyoh, Dickson. 'Community, citizenship and the politics of post-colonial Africa', in Ezekiel Kalipeni and Paul Zeleza (eds), *Sacred Spaces and Public Quarrels*. Africa World Press, Trenton, NJ, and Asmara, 1999.

Eyoh, Dickson. 'The Ethnic Question in African Democratization Experiences'. Paper presented at the 10th General Assembly of CODESRIA, Kampala, Uganda on 8—12 December, 2002.

Fabian, Johannes. *Power and Performance: Ethnographic Explorations through Proverbial Wisdom and Theater in Shaba, Zaire*. Madison: University of Wisconsin Press, 1990.

Fabian, Johannes. 'Popular Culture in Africa: Findings and Conjectures.' *AfricaJournal of the International African Institute* 48(4), 1978, pp 315-334.

Fairclough, N. *Discourse and Social Change*. Cambridge: Polity Press, 1992.

Ferguson, James. 'The Country and the City on the Copperbelt', in *Cultural Anthropology*, 7(1) 1992.

Finnegan, Ruth. *Oral Literature in Africa*. Oxford: Clarendon Press 1970.

Frederiksen, BodilFolke 'Joe, the Sweetest Reading in Africa: Documentation and Discussion of a Popular Magazine in Kenya' in Stephanie Newell's *Readings in African Popular Fiction*. Oxford: James Currey, 2002.

Frith, Simon. *Sound Effects: Youth Leisure and the Politics of Rock*. London: Constable, 1983.

Gaitho, Macharia, 'Swelling Phobia for Big Tribes: Love and Hate have Defined Relationship with Gĩkũyũ, Luo' in *Moi: End of an Era,* a special supplement of the *Daily Nation,* 24th December, 2002.

Garofalo, Reebee. (ed) *Rockin' the Boat: Mass Music Movements*. Boston, Mass.: South End Press, 1992.

Gecau, Kimani.' "The World has no Owner" – Popular Songs and Social Realities in Africa' in Vambe, Maurice .T. (ed) *Orality and Cultural Identities in Zimbabwe*. Gweru: Mambo Press, 2002.

Gecau, Kimani.. 'The 1980s Background to the Popular Political Songs of the Early 1990s in Kenya'in RinoZhuwarara, Kĩmani Gecau and Mariana Drag, (eds)*Media, Democratization and Identity*. Harare: Dept. of English, University of Zimbabwe, 1997.

Gecau, Kimani. 'Culture and the Tasks of Development in Africa: Lessons from the Kenyan Experience' in PrebenKaarsholm's (ed) *Cultural Struggle an Development in Southern Africa*. Harare: Baobab, 1991.

Gikandi, Simon, "The Politics and Poetics of National Formation, Recent African Writing", in Anna Rutherford (ed.), *From Commonwealth to Postcolonial*, Sydney, Dangaroo Press, 1992.

Gilroy, Paul. *The Black Atlantic: Modernity and Double Consciousness*. Cambridge, Massachusetts: Harvard University Press, 1993.

Graebner, Werner. (ed) *Sokomoko: Popular Culture in East Africa*. Amsterdam-Atlanta: GA, 1992.

Githinji, Peter. 'Bazes and Their Shibboleths: Lexical Variation and Sheng Speakers' Identity in Nairobi'*Nordic Journal of African Studies* 15(4): 443–472 (2006).

Githiora, Chege. 'Sheng: Peer language, Swahili dialect or emerging Creole?'*Journal of African Cultural Studies* 15(2) 2002, 159–181.

Githiora, Christopher. 'Recreating Discourse and Performance in Kenyan Urban Space through *Mũgithi*, Hip Hop and *Gĩcandĩ*'. *Journal of African Cultural Studies*, Volume 20, Number 1, June 2008, pp. 85-93(9).

Hall, Stuart. 'The Question of Cultural Identity', in *Modernity and its Futures*. S. Hall, D. Held & T. McGrew (eds). Cambridge: Polity Press, 1992.

Hanks, William. F. (1989) 'Text and Textuality', *Annual Review of Anthropology*, 18: 95–127.

Harker, David. "The Original Bob Cranky?" in *Folk Music Journal* 5:1 1985.

Haugerud, Angelique. *The Culture of Politics in Modern Kenya*. Cambridge: Cambridge University Press, 1995.

Hempstone, Smith. *The Rogue Ambassador: An African Memoir*. Sewanee: University of the South Press, 1997.

Hofmeyr, Isabel. 'Popular Literature in Africa: Post-Resistance Perspectives'. *Social Dynamics 30(2), 2004.*

Hofmeyr, Isabel, Joyce Nyairo and James Ogude. 'Who Can Bwogo Me?': Popular Culture in Kenya', in *Social Identities*, 9(3). 2003.

Hopton-Jones, Pamela. 'Introducing the Music of East Africa'. *Music Educators Journals* No 95 Vol 82 Issue 3.

Horner, Bruce and Thomas Swiss.*Key Terms in Popular Music and Culture*. Massachusetts: Blackwell Publishers Inc, 1999.

Human Rights Watch, *Kenya's Unfinished Democracy, A Human Rights Agenda for the New Government*. Vol. 14 (10A), December 2002.

Irele, Abiola. Editorial.*Research in African Literatures*. 32(2) 2001.

Jameson, Fredric. *The Ideologies of Theory Essays, 1971-1986: The Situations of Theory*. London: Routledge, 1988.

Jameson, Fredric. 'Modernism and Its Repressed: Robbe-Grillet as Anti-Colonialist'. *Diacritics,* Vol. 6, No. 2 (1976), pp. 7-14.

Jewsiewicki, Bogumil, and L. N'SandaBuleli. "Ethnicities as 'First Nations' of the Congolese Nation State: Some Preliminary Observations." *Ethnicity and Democracy in Africa.*Ed. Bruce Berman, Dickson Eyoh, and Will Kimlicka. Oxford: Currey, 2004.

Jewsiewicki, Bogumil. 'Popular Culture and Political Ideology' in *Encyclopedia of Africa South of The Sahara, Vol 3*. John Middleton, (ed) New York: Charles Scribner's, 1997.

Kaarsholm, Preben. *Cultural Struggle and Development in Southern Africa.* Harare: Baobab, 1991.

Kabira, Wanjiku Mukabi and Karega wa Mutahi. *Gĩkũyũ Oral Literature.*Nairobi: East African Educational Publishers, 1988.

Kagwanja, Peter. 'Facing Mount Kenya or Facing Mecca? The Mũngĩkĩ, Ethnic Violence and the Politics of the Moi Succession in Kenya 1987-2002'. *African Affairs* 102, 2003.

Kamawira, James (Kham). Editorial Cartoon. East African Standard. November 2nd 2003.

Kariuki, James. "'Paramoia': Anatomy of a Dictatorship in Kenya'. *Journal of Contemporary African Studies,* 14(1), 1996.

Kariuki, John, "Forget your Language and Lose your Culture" in *The East African,* 3rd March 2002.

Kariuki, John. 'Flashback to Praise Songs Era', in *The Sunday Nation*, November 3rd, 2002.

Kariuki, John. 'Out of Tune Mugabe Torments Musicians, in *The East African*, Monday, March 4, 2002.

Kariuki, John. 'Political Game a Test for Singers' in *The Sunday Nation,* January 28th, 2001.

Kariuki, John. 'Why Kenyan Musicians are Looking Back for Lyrical Inspiration'. *Sunday Nation*, September 6th, 1998.

Kasyoka, Diana, "KICC Right at the Centre of our History", in *Daily Nation*, 23rd May 2005.

Kavyu, P. N. *An Introduction to Kamba Music*. Nairobi: East African Literature Bureau, 1977.

Kavyu, P.N. "The Development of Guitar Music in Kenya." *Jazzforschung*10 (1978): 111–20.

Kenyatta, Jomo. *Facing Mount Kenya: The Tribal Life of the Gĩkũyũ*. London: Secker & Warburg, 1938.

Kiel, Charles. 'People's Music Comparatively: Style and Stereotype, Class and Hegemony', in *Dialectical Anthropology 10*. 1985.

Kituyi, Mukhisa, "Democracy, Why Kenyans Have given up the Struggle" in *The Sunday Nation,* 16th July 2000.

Kwaramba, Alice Dadirai. *Popular Music and Society: The Language of Protest in Chimurenga Music: The Case of Thomas Mapfumo in Zimbabwe.* IMK Report No. 24. University of Oslo, 1997.

Lodge, Tom. *'Newspapers as a Primary Source for Researchers in Political and Historical Studies'*. Seminar paper, University of the Witwatersrand, 2001.

Low, John. 'A History of Kenyan Guitar Music 1945-1980' in *African Music* 6 (2) 1982 pp 17-36.

MacGaffey, Janet and RémyBazenguissa-Ganga. *Congo-Paris: Transnational Traders on the Margins of the Law*. Oxford: James Currey, 2000.

Maina waKinyattĩ. *Kenya: A Prison Notebook*. London: Vita Books, 1996.

Maina waKinyattĩ. *Thunder From the Mountains: Mau Mau Patriotic Songs*. London: Zed Press, 1980.

Marangoly, George Rosemary. *The Politics of Home*. Cambridge. Cambridge University Press, 1996.

Martin, Denis-Constant. 'Music Beyond Apartheid?' in Garofalo, Reebee. (Ed) *Rockin' the Boat: Mass Music Movements*. Boston, Mass.: South End Press, 1992.

Masolo, D.A. 'Presencing the Past and Remembering the Present: Social Features of Popular Music in Kenya', in Ronald Radano and Philip Bohlman *Music and Racial Imagination*. Chicago: University of Chicago Press, 2000.

Matheson, Ishbel "Kenyans Dance against Graft" in *BBC News* 18th September 2001.

Maupeu, Hervé and Mbigua wa-Mingai. 'La Politique Des Bars Gĩkũyũ De Nairobi' in*Cahiers D'études Africaines* 2006/2 (n° 182)2006.pp313-331.

Mbembe, Achille. *On the Postcolony*. Berkeley: University of California Press, 2001.

Mbembe, Achille. 'Provisional Notes on the Postcolony', *Africa* 62(1), 1992.

Mbugua, Karanja. "Understanding the Ideology of Vernacular Broadcasting, Ethnicity and Class Tensions", *Expression Today,* 27[th]November 2000.

McQuail, Denis. *Mass Communication Theory: An Introduction*. London: Sage, 1993. 2[nd]edition.

Middleton, Richard. *Studying Popular Music*. Milton Keynes: Open University Press, 1990.

Miller, Norman N. *Kenya: The Quest for Prosperity*. Boulder: Westview Press, 1984.

Morson, Gary Saul and Caryl Emerson. *Mikhail Bakhtin: Creation of a Prosaics*. Stanford: Stanford University Press, 1990.

Morton, Andrew. *Moi: The Making of an African Statesman*. London: Michael O'Mara Books Ltd. 1998.

Mucoki, Mburu. *A Study of Themes in Kenya's Popular-Political Music in the Last 15 Years*. Unpublished Research Report. School of Journalism, University of Nairobi, 1992.

Muganda, Clay. ´Queen who's Worthy of the Title´, in the *Daily Nation,* 12th November 2004.

Muhoro, Mwangi. 'The Song-Narrative Construction of Oral History through the Gĩkũyũ Mũthĩrĩgũ and Mwomboko' in *Fabula: Journal of Folk-Tale Studies*. 38(3 &4), 1997.

Munene, Macharia. 'Hazards of Postmodern Colonialism in Kenya'. Draft Paper prepared for conference on the Political Economy of Kenya, Oxford University, May 27-28, 2004, Oxford, United Kingdom.

Munene, Macharia. 'The Colonial Policies of Segregating the Gĩkũyũ, 1920-1964' in *ChemChemi International Journal of Arts and Social Sciences*, Vol 2 (2), 2000.

Muriuki, Godfrey. *A History of the Kikuyu 1500-1900*. Nairobi: Oxford University Press, 1974.

Mutonya, Maina; Mwaniki Wanjohi, Sam Kiiru and John Kariuki. *Retracing Kikuyu Popular Music*. Nairobi: Ketebul Music, 2010.

Mutonya, Maina. 'Ethnic Identity and Stereotypes in Popular Music: *Mũgithi* Performance in Kenya', in Kimani Njogu and Herve Maupeu (Eds) *Songs and Politics in Eastern Africa*. Dar es Salaam: Mkuki na Nyota Publishers, 2007.

Mutonya, Maina. '*Mũgithi* Performance, Popular Music, Stereotypes and Ethnic Identity'.*Africa Insight* 35 (2) 2005: 53–60.

Mutonya, Maina. *The Laughing Cry. (Mwa)Kenya Prison Literature*. MA Research Report, University of the Witwatersrand, Johannesburg, 2001.

Mutonya, Mungai. "Redefining Nairobi's Streets: Study of Slang, Marginalization, and Identity," *Journal of Global Initiatives: Policy, Pedagogy, Perspective*: Vol. 2 (2), 2007. pp169-185.

Mwangi, Evan. 'Journal's Special Issue on Kenya Focuses on Culture'in the *Sunday Nation* online Edition of October 19th 2003.

Mwendwa, Emmanuel. "What DJs Must Do for Local Art", in *The East African Standard,* 21st May 2000.

Ndebele, Njabulo. *Rediscovery of the Ordinary: Essays on South African Literature and Culture*. Johannesburg: Cosaw, 1991.

Ndĩgĩrĩgĩ, Gĩcingiri. 'Kenyan Theatre after Kamĩrĩthũ' in *The Drama Review 43(2),* 1999.

Ndĩgĩrĩgĩ, Gĩcingiri. 'Kamarũ, Mwarimũ wa Mũingĩ', in *Mũtiiri 1(1)* 1994.

Negus, Keith. *Popular Music in Theory: An Introduction*. Hanover, NH: University Press of New England, 1997.

Nesbitt, Nick. 'African Music, Ideology and Utopia'.*Research in African Literatures* 32(2) 2001.

Newell, Stephanie, 'Paracolonial Networks': The Rise of Literary and Debating Societies in Colonial West Africa' in *Literary Culture in Colonial Ghana: 'How to Play the Game of Life'*. Bloomington: Indiana University Press, 2002.

Newell, Stephanie. *Ghanaian Popular Fiction: "Thrilling Discoveries in Conjugal Life" and Other Tales* Oxford: James Currey, 2000.

Ngaira, Amos, "One-man Guitarist Releases CD" in *Sunday Nation*, 19th January2003 .

Ngaira, Amos. 'The Growing *Mũgithi* Craze' in *Saturday Nation*, October 26th, 2002.

Ngaira, Amos. 'The Lure of Gospel Music'. *Saturday Nation*, June 22nd 2002.

Ngugi waThiong'o. *Moving the Centre: The Struggle for Cultural Freedoms*. London: James Currey, 1993.

Njogu, Kimani. 'The Culture of Politics and Ethnic Nationalism in Central Province and Nairobi' in Marcel Rutten, Alamin Mazrui and Francois Grignon, *Out for the Count: The 1997 General Elections and Prospects for Democracy in Kenya*. Kampala: Fountain Publishers, 2001.

Njogu, Kimani, 'Popular Culture: Eastern and Central Africa' in *Encyclopedia of Africa South of the Sahara Vol 3*. John Middleton, (Ed) New York: Charles Scribner's, 1997.

Nyairo, Joyce W. 'Contesting Domestic Space(s): *Mutenguano* and The Cultural and National Politics of Urban Pastimes' paper read at Cadbury Conference on *'Cultural Nationalism and Social Critique'*, University of Birmingham, 13-14 May, 2005.

Nyairo, Joyce. "Reading the referents, The Ghost of America in Contemporary Kenyan Popular Music", *Scrutiny* 29, no. 1, 2004.

Nyairo, Joyce W. and James Ogude. 'Popular Music and the Negotiation of Contemporary Kenyan Identity: The Example of Nairobi City Ensemble', in *Social Identities*, 9(3) 2003.

Nyambura, Phyllis. 'The Good, the Bad and the Ugly.' *Saturday Nation*, December 27th 2003.

Nzewi, Meki, Israel Anyahuru and Tom Ohiaraumuna. 'Beyond Song Texts. The Lingual Fundamentals of African Drum Music', in *Research in African Literatures* 32(2), 2001.

Odhiambo, E.S. Atieno. 'Hegemonic Enterprises and Instrumentalities of Survival: Ethnicity and Democracy in Kenya' in *African Studies* 61(2), 2002.

Odhiambo, E.S. Atieno. 'Kula Raha: Gendered Discourses & the Contours of Leisure in Nairobi, 1946-1963,' The Urban Experience in Eastern Africa, 18th Century-1980s'Conference Paper, Nairobi, Kenya (1-4 Jul 2001).

Ogola, George. 'Nyayo Show Lives Up to Expectations' in the *East African Standard*, Friday, June 4, 1999.

Ogot, Behwell A. and W.R. Ochieng'. *Decolonization & Independence in Kenya 1940-93*. London : J. Currey, 1995.

Ogot, Bethwell A. 'Politics, Culture and Music in Central Kenya, a Study of Mau Mau Hymns', in *Kenya Historical Review: Special Issue on Some Perspectives on the Mau Mau Movement* (5.2), 1977.

Ogude, James, & Joyce Nyairo (eds.) *Urban Legends, Colonial Myths: Popular Culture and Literature in East Africa*. Trenton NJ and Asmara: Africa World Press, 2007.

Ogude, James 'The Truths of the Nation' and the Changing Image of Mau Mau in Kenyan Literature' in E.S. Atieno Odhiambo and John Lonsdale (eds) *Mau Mau and Nationhood: Arms, Authority & Narration*. Oxford: James Currey, 2003.

Okwonkwo, Juliet. 'Popular Urban Fiction and Cyprian Ekwensi', in *A Comparative History of Literatures in European Languages*. 1986,

Olaniyan, Tejumola. 'The Cosmopolitan Nativist and the Antimonies of Postcolonial Modernity'.*Research in African Literatures* 32(2) 2001.

Omwa, Obara. 'When the Village Comes to Town'.*Saturday Nation*, October 18th 2003.

Ondego, Ogova. "Will the World Listen to Music "Made in Kenya*?" The East African*, 9th April 2001.

Ondego, Ogova, "Identity Crisis Facing Top African Musicians", *The Sunday Nation, Lifestyle*, Nairobi, 7th May 2000.

Osamba, Joshia. 'Violence and the Dynamics of Transition: State, Ethnicity and Governance in Kenya', in *Africa Development*, XXVI: 1& 2, 2001.

Outa, George Odera. "Lysistrata in Nairobi: Performing the Power of Womanhood in the Post-colony" in *African Studies*, 58(2), 1999.

Palmberg, Mai and Kirkegaard, Annemette. *Playing with Identities in Contemporary Music in Africa.*Uppsala: Nordic African Institute, 2002.

Parkes, Peter. 'Personal and Collective Identity in Kalasha Song Performance: The Significance of Music-making in a Minority Enclave'; in Martin Stokes, (ed) *Ethnicity, Identity and Music: The Musical Construction of Place*. Oxford: Berg, 1994.

Paterson, Doug. "The Life and Times of Kenyan Pop" in *World Music: The Rough Guide. Volume I.* Broughton, Simon Mark Ellingham and Richard Trillo, with Orla Duane and Vanessa Dowell. (eds) London: Rough Guides, 1999.

Powell, Chris and George E.C Paton (eds.). *Humour in Society: Resistance and Control.* London: Macmillan Press, 1988.

Pugliese, Cristiana. *Complementary or Contending Nationhoods? Gĩkũyũ Political Pamphlets and Songs: 1945-1952*, Nairobi: I.F.R.A. Working Papers, June 1993.

Pugliese, Cristiana. *Author, Publisher and Gĩkũyũ Nationalist: The Life and Writings of Gakaara wa Wanjau*. Bayreuth: Bayreuth African Studies 37, in cooperation with Nairobi: I.F.R.A (InstitutFrançais de Recherché en Afrique, 1995.

Ranger, Terence. 'Religion and Everyday Life in Contemporary Zimbabwe' in Preben Kaarsholm, ed. *Cultural Struggle and Development in Southern Africa*. London: James Currey, 1991.

Rugene, Njeri and Mugo Njeru. 'A Hero's Homecoming', *Sunday Nation*, December 15th 2002.

Rutherford, Anna. (ed) *From Commonwealth to Post-Colonial*. Sydney: Dangaroo Press, 1992.

Schatzberg, Michael G. *The Dialectics of Oppression in Zaire*. Bloomington and Indianapolis: Indiana University Press, 1988.

Schlesinger, Minky. *Nightingales and Nice-time Girls: The Story of Township Women and Music (1900-1960)*. Johannesburg: Viva, 1993.

Schmidt, Siegmar and Gichira Kibara. *Kenya on the Path toward Democracy? An Interim Evaluation: A Qualitative Assessment of Political Developments in Kenya between 1990 and June 2002*. Nairobi: Konrad Anenauer Foundation, 2002.

Scott, James C. *Weapons of the Weak: Everyday Forms of Peasant Resistance*. New Haven: Yale University Press 1985.

Scott, James C. *Domination and the Arts of Resistance*.New Haven: Yale University Press, 1990.

Shepherd, John. *Music as Social Text*. Cambridge: Polity Press, 1991.

Sicherman, Carol. 'Kenya, Creativity and Political Repression: The Confusion of Fact and Fiction', in *Race and Class* 37(4) 1996.

Smith, Susan. 'Soundscape' in *Area*, 26, 1994.

Stapleton, Chris and Chris May. *African All Stars: The Pop Music of a Continent*. London: Grafton, 1989.

Stephens, Simon. 'Kwaito', in Sarah Nutall and Cheryl-Anne Michael (eds) *Sense of Culture: South African Cultural Studies*. Oxford: Oxford University Press, 2000, pp 256-273.

Stokes, Martin. *Ethnicity, Identity and Music: The Musical Construction of Place*. Oxford: Berg, 1994.

Storey, John. *Cultural Studies and the Study of Popular Culture*. Edinburgh: Edinburgh University Press, 1996.

Street John. *Politics and Popular Culture*. Cambridge: Polity Press, 1997.

Street, John. *Rebel Rock: The Politics of Popular Music*. Oxford: B. Blackwell, 1986.

Strinati, Dominic. *An Introduction to Studying Popular Culture* London; New York: Routledge, 2000.

Strinati, Dominic. *An Introduction to Theories of Popular Culture*. London: Routledge, 1995.

Turino, Thomas. *Nationalists, Cosmopolitans, and Popular Music in Zimbabwe*. Chicago: University of Chicago Press, c2000.

Verjee, Zain. "Kenya, Journey through a Rhythm Nation", in *BBC News*, 30th August 1999.

Wambua, Sammy. 'Songsters Outdid themselves in their Rush to Praise the President's Regime' in the *Daily Nation*, December 24th, 2003.

Wanjohi, Gerald Joseph. *Under One Roof: Gĩkũyũ Proverbs Consolidated*. Nairobi: Paulines Publications Africa, 2001.

Wanjohi, Gerald Joseph. *The Wisdom and Philosophy of African Proverbs: The Gĩkũyũ World-View*. Nairobi: Paulines Publications Africa, 1997

Wanyeki, Lynne Muthoni. "Kenya-Population, Church Burns Condoms and AIDS Materials" *InterPress News Service (IPS)*, 5thSeptember de 1996.

Waterman, Christopher Allan. *Jùjú: A Social History and Ethnography of an African Popular Music*. Chicago: University of Chicago Press, 1990.

Waweru, Kiundu, "*Mũgithi*, Scholar Unravels Popular Music Roots and Lewd Lyrics" en *The Standard*, 10th March 2011.

Wekesa, Wafula Peter. 'The Politics of Marginal Forms: Popular Music, Cultural Identity and Political Opposition in Kenya'. Paper presented at *CODESRIA* General Assembly, Kampala, Uganda, December 2002.

Werbner, Richard. *Memory and the Postcolony: African Anthropology and the Critique of Power*. London; New York: Zed Books, 1998.

Werbner, Richard and Terence Ranger.*Postcolonial Identities in Africa*. London and New Jersey: Zed Books, 1996.

Online Sources

https://www.cia.gov/library/publications/the-world-factbook/geos/ke.html (Accessed 7th March 2010).

http://www.knbs.or.ke/docs/PresentationbyMinisterforPlanningrevised.pdf (accessed 7th March 2010).

www.transparency.org (10th October 2002).

http://www.enchanted-landscapes.com/k_music/3_music_dkkamau.htm (Accessed 25th July 2009).